Who Am I?

Q & A

Who Am I?

Q & A

Ann Shaw

© 2025 Ann Shaw

First Edition: March 2025

ISBN: 978-1-7393093-1-2

Published by "Who Am I? Books"

www.whoamibook.co.uk

annshaw@whoamibook.co.uk

www.annshaw.space

annshawspace@gmail.com

All rights reserved. No part of this publication may be reproduced, stored in a retrieval system, translated or transmitted in any form or by any means, electronic, mechanical, photo-copying, recording, or otherwise, without prior written permission from the agent, publisher or author.

"True spirituality has nothing to do with holiness or piety.

Spirituality has one purpose, and one purpose alone, which is to erase illusion and establish your original identity –

that you are Ultimate Truth."

Shri Ramakant Maharaj

*"There is an inbuilt yearning in the heart,
a hunger to know the infinite."*

*"The divine romance means devotion to your
Beloved Source
through Self-attentiveness."*

*"You fell in love with the impermanent, now
fall in love with the permanent."*

Ann Shaw

Contents

Preface   *ii*

Introduction   *iii*

Part One Q & A's on Advaita Vedanta/
Non-Duality   *1*

Part Two Q & A's on Advaita Vedanta/
Non-Duality & the Lineage Teachings   *134*

Further Reading / Resources   *254*

About the Author   *255*

Preface

The Q & A's contained in this book first appeared in 2023-24, as a series of "10-minute videos". The questions address the various practices which readers were introduced to in the first book, *Who Am I?* such as Self-enquiry, Meditation, Mantra and Kirtan/*Bhajans*, as well as the subjects of Self-Realization, Devotion and many others.

All questions are body-based questions which, eventually, need to be discarded. However, in the early stages of deprogramming, they need to be answered, otherwise, they will remain obstacles to one's progress.

Part One covers general questions about Advaita Vedanta/Non-Duality. Part Two introduces readers to the (little known in the West), "Inchegiri Navnath Sampradaya Lineage" and addresses questions about Advaita Vedanta, in the context of this lineage. Ann Shaw's final Teacher and Master, Ramakant Maharaj is part of this lineage. Bhausaheb Maharaj is the head of this lineage. Other great Masters include Nisargadatta Maharaj, Ranjit Maharaj, and their Master, Siddharameshwar Maharaj. Here, readers will learn about the alchemical relationship between the Guru and disciple and various practices, such as reciting the *Naam Mantra*, *Guru Bhakti* and *Devotion After Liberation*.

Introduction

This knowledge is the highest and most direct because we start with the Reality, our Reality, as the Absolute! Nothing less! The teaching that we are the Absolute is not a premise, but a Reality. Our stance is prior to beingness, prior to consciousness. It is our permanent position, nothing less. What does this mean? It means that the process we are undergoing will take us back home to where we came from, namely the "Stateless State", where there is no knowledge, no words, no language, no duality, no you, no me, no nothing.

Prior to the manifestation of the body form, we existed as one Essence, formless, thoughtless, silent, without words, without husbands or wives, families, without religions, views, beliefs etc. We had no identity. There was no spirituality either. Everything is an illusion, including spirituality, which is only used to remove the thorn of ignorance. Once this has been done, we dispose of both thorns.

Our path has nothing to do with what we believe in, or causes we adhere to, or beliefs we have developed in this life. Why? Because these illusory layers only appeared after beingness. They were all learned. They are all part of our conditioning which the ego-mind has built up as part of its pseudo identity. Therefore, it is inevitable that the process we are undergoing will challenge and clash with any kind of belief we still hold dear. Be prepared to discard them all because they are not part of your true nature. They are not part of who you are.

This process is one of subtraction, not addition. We are not adding anything new because everything is within us already. Our only business is to uncover all the layers of illusion that have obscured our real nature. We are removing everything we have learned, accumulated and been influenced by, over a lifetime. These Q & A's will help remove the noisy clutter of concepts, doubts and fears, clearing the space that will bring you closer to Reality, closer to finding the wordless answer to "Who am I?"

Part One: Q & A's on Advaita Vedanta/Non-Duality

Self-Enquiry

Q. I do practice Self-enquiry and I know that I am not my name, sex, body, mind, feelings, etc. The penny is beginning to drop that I am an illusion. But when I am with my family, I think that my mother is real, my sister is real, and in the process, I guess I forget to Self-enquire. Instead, I behave as if I am truly a son and brother!

A. You are not alone in falling into this trap. When it comes to our close family and friends, it is not so easy to apply the teachings. You need to continue with Self-enquiry. Also, it is a good idea to listen each day to the beautiful *bhajan Chidananda,* composed by the great philosopher and saint, Adi Shankaracharya. Let the words sink in! *Chidananda* contains the essence of Advaita using the *neti neti* approach: I am not this, I am not that... including,

"I am not father, mother, hence no birth.

I am not brother, nor friend, nor guru nor aspirant.

I am eternal bliss, I am Shiva.

I am eternal bliss, I am Shiva."

Q. How to ensure that repeatedly asking, "Where was this thought prior to beingness?", remains as Self-enquiry, instead of it becoming a kind of *japa* or repetition? Do we ask only one question? "Who is asking this, who is thinking this?" or as Bhagavan Ramana sometimes asked, "Who is sad and unhappy?". Or as you said, restrict it to one simple question? But how to guard from it becoming a mantra? And kindly elaborate on how to stay in reality? Is it remaining in being after a spell of arresting thoughts at the root, or a separate gentle effort to be without thoughts?

A. Keep it simple. You only use the question re: thoughts, as soon as you catch yourself falling into the illusion by taking that thought for real. Put simply, when you are not drawn into thoughts, you are in reality. Then with practice, the space between thoughts enlarges, until it becomes the thoughtless state.

Practice remaining as the witness of the dream, by staying more detached from daily life. As the witness, you stand one step removed from the dream, always knowing that "you are not of the world".

Q. This morning I asked myself the question: Is the conscious one or the one who focuses on the "Invisible Listener" the same thing? I.E., the Invisible Listener is aware of himself and concentrates on himself. Right?

A. There is only one always. No duality! Whenever duality appears, illusion is present. Don't let words or intellectualization come in the way. Keep it simple.

Q. I realized that my goal is not to depart this world or banish the ego which doesn't exist anyway, except in my mind, but to fully live in both worlds. To have a successful life in this playground as a human, yet still know who I am in spirit! I know I am nothing. However, the question I have for myself is: Is my understanding of myself as nothing a true direct experience, or is it just more intellectual concepts I have gathered along the way?

It seems that the problem with all I'm telling you is that most of it is still just a part of the intellect. These are all fancy notions, concepts and ideas. I would like a simple practice that directly relates to this direction that I'm going. Of course I'm not really going anywhere, because there's nowhere to go. It's all right here.

A. Your message is replete with "I this, I that". Our goal is to remove the "I", die to the "I", the ego and wake up from the long dream of life. Be liberated before the body expires! There are so many teachers who just pile knowledge on top of the ego. It is never ending. The knowledge is never established or made one's own! What is missing is a cleansing or purification process. Self-Enquiry is essential as well as absorbing the knowledge of who you are, in essence.

You say you wish to keep your feet in both worlds. There is only one Reality - the world is an illusion. When all the layers of programming, conditioning and superimpositions we have been subjected to have been removed, then your true nature will begin to emerge: That which you have always been, That which has never been touched by the world. That which is immutable!

When the Conviction that you are unborn is established, you won't need to live in both worlds because there will be Self-fulfilment, causeless happiness and the certainty that you are immortal. You say you are not keen on reading books, that your only interest is in knowledge. I suggest you read *Selfless Self* first. I will also email you a few *bhajans*/devotional songs which are in essence, non-dual. Their purpose is to bring the knowledge down from the head to the heart. Dry, intellectual knowledge is useless! After you finish reading *Selfless Self*, we will move on to a meditation technique

Theory is useless

Q. I am not getting any results yet.

A. You should not be doing the practice with results in mind – if I do X then I will get Y. And it is not true to say there have not been any obvious changes. Leave that awareness to me for the time-being! After reading *Timeless Years* there was a noticeable opening up of the heart within you. Our bond grew deeper and your devotion increased and continues to express itself in your messages to me. In conclusion, Ultimate Reality will not emerge until all body-based illusion has been erased. The "I", the "ego" is still there, so, how can you expect Self-Realization?

At this point in the process, you need to have complete faith in the practice, that it is working, in spite of what the mind is telling you. Stop listening to the thoughts of there not being any results, as this will have a negative effect on your going forward. And it can, if you're not careful, become another block. As Maharaj says, Self-Realization takes different lengths of time, depending on your spiritual maturity.

Also, I feel you need to get in touch more with your inner drive to find truth, to know who you are. Remember that liberation is from you, not of you. You use the future tense, saying, "I will have to say goodbye to my identity", when all is happening in the present as process. Also, you say you are theoretically ready. Once again, the mind is talking. Theory is useless and the "I's" are evident. I am theoretically ready for this, but still nothing happens. Who is saying this? Self-enquire! Mentally you may know some of the teachings but they have not been accepted or lived, i.e., known pragmatically.

There should not be any distinction made between the periods of practice and the rest of the day. You are compartmentalizing the practice and your work/family life when the practice is a 24 hour practice, nothing less. When you're at work, you should practice remaining in the witness mode as much as possible, while carrying out your duties. Remain detached, not letting yourself take it all for real. Be aware of when your attention leaves your centre, when it leaves Selfless Self and you get immersed in illusion.

With practice, you should be able to stay one removed from what is happening around you. Watch yourself from a distance, witness yourself playing a part in the movie. It looks like you're still caught up in the movie and taking the dream for reality. How seriously are you about Self-Realization? Yes, you carry out the practice, but how involved are you? Involvement means remembering your identity 24/7, not just during the practice. And in order for this to happen, you need to absorb the teachings more. Shri Siddharameshwar Maharaj says you should know the teachings inside out, so that you never get caught out by the world, unawares. If you know the teachings completely, then they are always to hand, leaving no opening for you to "fall into the ditch" - to quote Maharaj - because you know what to do before that happens.

Now for the positives: you're a very good devotee. You follow all that I say. You're open and honest and do not conceal anything from me. Finally, here is your prescription: Follow the instructions and take the medicine, all of it. Taking into account that your days are full and busy, your weak point is still the knowledge. I would give less time to the *bhajans* and more time to the knowledge, as it is still not absorbed. The *bhajans* are used to help absorb the knowledge, but if there are holes in the knowledge, then the *bhajans* are not so pressing.

I feel that you've not read and studied *Selfless Self* enough. I recommend one chapter a day. Sit with it, churn it over and over again and again, throughout the day. Meditating on the knowledge means sitting with it, dwelling on it, and if you do this regularly, you will be able to absorb the knowledge. Then the mind will quieten down. Let me remind you of the process, the Mantra helps to dissolve you. When you hear the vibration and meaning of "*I am Brahman, Brahman I am*", this helps you to remember your true identity. But by itself, it's not enough. Without a true and deep grasp of the knowledge, the false knowledge you have of yourself will linger. All the remnants will not be swept away. Our growing Conviction that we are That, will bring us closer to Self-Realization. When we bow to the divinity of the Masters, we are bowing to that one same divinity in us.

You are not a slave

Q. I am trying to keep up the practice and meditate 2 hours a day. But then problems come along, people dump things on me, difficulties at work and then I feel as if I am back to square one. I don't think I'm strong enough to overcome all these.

A. Who is saying this? Do not be a slave of your mind, listening and reacting to everything and everyone around you. You are not a slave, you are a Master. It is up to you whether you carry on listening to all the illusory thoughts and to others. Use discernment and separate out illusion from reality. Train yourself not to give you attention to these problems and difficulties. Use discrimination actively! Anchor yourself in Reality, in Selfless Self. You may not be able to control what comes your way, but you have total control of how you respond. Will you let this or that illusion sting you, drag you into the ditch, or will you remain as the witness and not be touched? Accept your Reality, stay with Reality and with courage and determination refuse to leave your centre. You have the power! Convince yourself of that and stay with the Truth that you are. Keep reminding yourself when old habits and patterns appear, that there is nothing except Selfless Self and you are That!

Q. I don't understand why there are some people who follow the lineage and then post videos of American charlatans, who profess to be gurus asking for $3300 dollars per person for Satsang. Often some are also Indians who should have a more complete culture than us Westerners, at least of the sacred scriptures. Shree Ramakant was right about everything. Every day they contact me privately to tell me how I should follow my sadhana, ask who my teacher is. Pandits who ask me for money to do rituals for luck and money and punctually I find myself receiving curses or bad words from them. There are many disciples in America who give Guru Mantra to everyone without permission. I humbly admit that I get angry because they are missing the respect to the Saint…

A. Stop right there! However angry you may feel about this, it is not your business. Try to ignore it. Don't be distracted. And keep your attention on your Self. Remember that if you let these things affect you, you are again falling into the trap, of taking illusion for reality. And don't be tricked by the spiritual ego either. Whatever goes on outside of you is not your business.

No-thing

Q. A question has arisen in meditation: If everything comes out of nothing and dissolves back into nothing, what is the purpose of enlightenment in this something?

A. You are an actor in this world. Through enlightenment you realize you are the director. The purpose of enlightenment is to wake up from the dream and realize that you are the Ultimate Reality. Although the actor and the director are both concepts, the director rightly infers that you are in charge. You are the only Power that makes everything happen.

Q. Could you clarify the quote "Apart from Selfless Self there is no *Atman*, no *Brahman*, etc?

A. Seekers think or believe that *Atman/Brahman* or the Reality is separate from them. When Maharaj emphasizes that there is nothing except Selfless Self, he means that you are that Selfless Self, *Atman* or *Brahman*. That nothing exists apart from the Reality that you are.

Prior to Beingness

Q. In *Selfless Self,* Ramakant Maharaj says that if you're not aware of yourself prior to beingness, then something seems to appear in nothing. Nothing takes itself for the something because it does not know any better. And in this case, the something is the body, and therefore, it immediately identifies with the body. I understand it in this way: if the Presence is not aware of itself prior to beingness then incarnation occurs, another dream arises and everywhere in the books it is said that the Presence in principle is not aware of itself, just as the sky does not know that it is the sky. So, I'm trying to figure out: Is this a contradiction or a misinterpretation? It's just that if realization is a state before beingness in which you don't know yourself, then, what's the point?

Let's say, the fact of non-existence scares me. Non-existence is not in the manifestation in which we are used to seeing the worldly life etc. But in general, the very fact of not being aware of your Presence, it is clear that self-examination and the question, "who is afraid of this?" go begging here. But I still want to try and understand and get the essence behind these words of Maharaj - if it is of course possible. For example, after your body expires, will you also not be aware of yourself, as it was before beingness? Or will the state still be different from the state that was before being this without awareness, since you became aware of yourself during life?

A. So your understanding is correct about prior to beingness. And then there is manifestation and identification with the body-form. There is no misinterpretation! Let's keep it simple. Supposing we have millions of incarnations and during each one of them, let's call them dreams, we don't wake up, we don't Self-realize. The body expires and then we return to prior to beingness again, but never wiser than before. Then again, there's another dream, but say, this time it's your last dream. This time you wake up! So, waking up is the point, otherwise we go round and round and round on the never-ending wheel like robotic idiots. How do you wake up? By realizing that you are not the body-mind! By removing all the layers. All these layers are composed of knowledge, worldly, man-made knowledge or add-ons to our true nature. During the process of Self-Realization, there is the realization that you are eternal, that you have always existed. You realize that you were never the form, but formless.

Logically, following this, you realize there is no you, and therefore, no you to know anything. You are beyond knowing and unknowing. Your eternal Essence between the state of ignorance in between incarnations and the stateless state of self-realization, is that after realization the cycle has ended. The cycle is broken. You are permanently free. Your work is done here on earth because you have fulfilled the goal.

In answer to your question, the state prior to beingness before realization is of course different because there is still ignorance or lack of enlightenment. You mentioned the fear of non-existence, too, but there is no such thing. We have always existed and we will ever exist in Essence, Energy, Power, Eternal Reality, Source, call it what you will. And that Source is beyond definition. *Brahman, Paramatman* or we can say Eternal Truth, Eternal love, Eternal Light, Eternal Bliss. You cannot know with the limited mind. You can only guess until it occurs. That is why Maharaj tells the story of someone shouting up to another who's standing at the top of a mountain. He says, "What is it like up there?" The man at the top says, "You will have to come up and see for yourself".

When awakening happens, knowing and being merge. The Stateless State is beyond awareness, beyond words. The former you has dissolved. When that has taken place, then who is aware? We cannot even use words to describe that which is prior to words. What we do know is that the Self-Realized *Jnanis,* the Presence of these Gurus like Nisargadatta and Ramakant etc., continues to be available to us here.

All concepts are illusion

Q. I am convinced there is destiny at work.

A. Who is convinced? Everything is illusion; every concept is an illusion. Where was the concept of destiny prior to beingness? It was not there. Therefore, destiny is an illusory concept that you need to let go of along with the rest of them. The bottom line is that everything is an illusion, every concept, without exception. The process you're undergoing is about dissolving everything you believe to be true. Removing the attachments, removing all the positions and stances you have taken up in life.

Q. The way I see it is I still believe there is such a thing as destiny.

A. I have already responded and told you that destiny is a concept. Let it go! You're undergoing a purification process. Once it has come to an end, there will be a shift in your perception. The way you view everything will change because you will no longer be in the picture. And when you're no longer there, everything will be viewed from the perspective of Oneness.

Presence

Q. I have two queries. When we say Presence before being - since even our childhood memories are hazy, how can we have an inkling of what we were before being? Is it akin to the deep sleep state? Second, when illusion is mentioned, probably it means everything except the presence is an illusion, including our own *sadhana*. So, we need not worry about our material happenings. Yet, somehow, we have to play the game of life and also sincerely practice the teachings. Can you give some more pointers to understand the presence before being, etc?

A. You cannot use the mind, to try and grasp or understand that which is prior to, and beyond the mind. You can get an inkling through our *neti neti* practice, by finding out everything about yourself that you are not. And then, what is left, is what you are.

I once asked Maharaj to elaborate on "Your presence was there prior to beingness", and after a moment of silence, he said: "That is enough!" meaning that all we can say about Presence, using words and the mind, is pointless because that Stateless State is prior to language! It is the mind's habit of thinking it can know the unlimited with the limited mind and that is impossible! Re: illusion, illusion refers to everything except that Presence. Our *sadhana*, too, is an illusion, but a necessary one. It is the secondary thorn that removes the primary thorn of "I am the body".

Q. I do not yet understand how my Presence and your Presence can be the same presence? In my case, the spirit became associated with this body specifically and can only experience anything through this particular body born in 1982. All the while, that same Presence is also looking at itself through your senses, through your mind. But from here, there is nothing but my senses and my mind. When Maharaj says that before the body you were formless, does that mean I was formless for all eternity before this body was born? Why did my Presence have to wait for a specific human organism before it clicked? Was it not also there as the Presence behind your body, Maharaj's body, Napoleon's body and everyone else who ever lived? And if so, why does Maharaj so often say, that before and after the body form, there is nothing whatsoever?

A. When we talk about Presence. we are referring to the Power, the Energy, the One Essence of which we are all a part. You are using the mind to try and work it out, which only keeps you in duality. This knowledge is all about nonduality, the Reality that is prior to and beyond the mind. There is only one Reality, not two, therefore, there is only one Presence. When the formless took form, when Spirit clicked with the body and then in your case, that body was given a specific name, so, you started to believe that you were this body-mind complex. You were separated from Source, from the One Source.

We were all separated from the one Source and because you were separated - not in essence, but by temporarily taking form, you believed yourself to be this body form and took yourself and the world for real. It is the same story for me. When the formless became form, I, too, forgot about my true identity and believed in the illusory story which I was fed and nurtured on.

You say you cannot see anything but your own senses and mind, but when you Self-enquire and through a process of *neti neti,* find out what you are not - and all that you thought you were was illusion - then you will discard these layers of conditioning, and eventually, reconnect with Source. You will conclude that everything is an illusion: you and the world and you will realize that you were and you are not separate. There is only Oneness. The idea of separation, individuality etc., was all an illusion. I could say more, but for now it is enough.

Before the body you were formless. If you can conceive that, in order to wake up from the dream that you're the body mind, countless so-called births have been taken, and each time you get closer to realizing your true nature. You are formless in eternity, prior to all the incarnations. If you awaken this time around, then no need for any more. In conclusion, your Presence did not wait for this specific one and only incarnation, it has taken form many times, with many different names ascribed to you. Your Presence ever existed; it has and will always be there like the sky, free of an I, omnipresent! So, yes! You're a part of the one and only Presence, as is everyone else. Maharaj says there is nothing, meaning no before and after the body form. Here in the context of no mind, no body, no thoughts, no world, no nothing, everything comes from nothing and returns to nothing. The apparent something that comes out of nothing is actually nothing, as the world is the projection of our Presence. I trust this offers some clarity.

Q. I thank you for the clarity. What is been conveyed by your words, like those of Maharaj is subtler than the literal meaning of the words. The analytical mind wants to put Reality into categories and it decides how these categories are allowed to relate to each other based on logic. The mystery of the formless self is prior to logic. The formless is expressed as form in seemingly multiple, simultaneous ways, without ever being other than oneness itself. Yet this, too, is a conception, an idea with certain boundaries rooted in the body. Even if I don't understand something intellectually, that doesn't matter. The intellect came along with the body and operates for the body's benefit. My unidentified, nonverbal non-conceptual self has no confusion.

Q. From where I stand, you are able to function normally. How can this be, when you are no longer the mind?

A. Some people think that Self-Realization means you become some kind of paralyzed entity of bliss. Throughout our lives, we have falsely believed that it is the mind that makes us function and operate in the world. We are so proud of that! Yet all along, it is the energy behind, the Presence, the power, call it what you will, that makes functioning possible. When the mind drops back into Source, everything will happen, spontaneously. The true engine in life will take over and do everything much better, than we could ever do!

Q. I am no longer interested in relationships, but I think it would be nice to have a companion to journey with. Is it possible to be in a relationship that is non dualistic and if so, how would that look like?

A. If a couple is interested in Nonduality and putting it into practice in their daily life, then yes, it is not only possible, but it will be very beautiful and rewarding. If the couple is engaged in removing the false identity and uncovering the one Reality, then there is, let us call it, no "delusionship" at play, but rather, a recognition of "oneship". With the understanding that there is not two, but only oneness, just Presence being with Presence, then what transpires is expansion and freedom, a deepening and elevating sharing of love. That love is not coming from an ego that is looking to get something. The love is coming from simply bathing in the Presence. From Presence to Presence.

Emotions

Q. I am looking at how I can control anger?

A. When the body responds to old conditioning then the answer is - don't control it! You know it is meaningless, so, just let it out! We already touched on this! Let the feeling pass and with practice, there will be fewer moments of anger because you will find less and less to be angry about. The great Masters appear to express anger but it does not mean anything. They are just making noises, unworthy of attention!

Q. I thought I was making progress, but now I am depressed again! Maybe I should do some voluntary work?

A. There is no person who is depressed. Instead of looking to lift the depression which is not real, you should be Self-enquiring to dissolve these illusions of believing in a person who is depressed. Where was your depression prior to beingness? Voluntary work is only a distraction, not a solution, for eradicating the illusion.

You see how you vacillate between telling me one minute, that the energy is palpable, asking if you are coming close to Spontaneous Conviction? And then, you suddenly indulge in the concept of depression again! You are supposed to be the witness of yourself and your illusory day-to-day ebbing and flowing! The depression is something that needs to be discarded, along with the other layers upon your Presence. The Mantra will help and is helping to reduce these negative waves of depression. From where I stand, they are not as frequent as before. Now they are more of a habit for you to let go of! We get attached to behaviour, both good and bad. What do you have to be depressed about, when the process of *neti neti* is well underway and you have had real glimpses of "I"?

You also need to absorb the knowledge in the books *Selfless Self* and *Who am I?* Listen and let it penetrate the multilayers of illusion. The knowledge continuously emphasizes that you and everything else are illusory. Only That which underlies all is Reality! So, why are you still harping on about depression!! It has become a habit, a bad friend which was perhaps a response to unhappy situations before, but is now no longer appropriate or relevant!

Again, I reiterate, where was your depression prior to beingness? I am reminding you to not give it your attention. In other words, don't feed it! "Ultimate Reality will not emerge until all body-based knowledge has dissolved". This includes "depression". In *Who am I?* you are guided and shown different ways of not giving attention to these base moods and feelings, so, why are you indulging again? Keep your attention on the Reality, Selfless Self, the Power, Energy, Source that you are, the Light that is behind, that empowers everything. Pull your socks up! Don't be a mouse, be a lion! Have a beautiful day. You are blessed, so, come out of the murky ditch. Remove the clouds and turn your face to the sun. Love and peace.

Let the process unfold spontaneously

Q. I still feel depressed and sad sometimes, even though I have been practicing for some months now.

A. Who is counting? A few months is nothing! Time is a concept. Deprogramming will take as long as it needs. Don't count the months! You have been programmed over a lifetime. You cannot expect total transformation overnight. We only feel depressed or sad if we think we are somebody, if we take our feelings and the ups and downs of life for real. When, through the process of dissolving, you know that you do not exist as a person and your true nature is revealed, then you will be liberated from your small self, the ego-mind. You will know that the reality that you are is all that is, therefore… who is sad, who is depressed? The result will be causeless, permanent happiness, peace and no death. Who can die when you are unborn!

Q. As you know, my outer life is depressing. Now the depressive feelings seem to have intensified, causing me more distress. What does it mean? I guess I need to persist, come what may? And till whatever time it takes, be driven by Maharaj's assurances?

A. The Mantra will clear out everything, consciously and unconsciously, while you are awake, dreaming or asleep. It means it is doing its job! Ignore the thoughts and let the process unfold spontaneously. All thought is unreal. The thinker is unreal. Keep up the practice with faith and determination. You are doing great! Be courageous! All is well, where it counts. Don't let the thoughts or feelings touch you. You are neither!

Every transient thing is illusory

Q. Is anger an impediment in the process of Self-Realization and if yes, how to get rid of anger?

A. All the emotions as we know, all thought, all emotions, all feelings, everything that's going on in the mind body are illusory. Maharaj refers to anger as just noises that emerge from us, akin to barking dogs. We shouldn't give much attention to the emotions whether they're anger, fear, depression or sadness because we know that all emotions are transient. They appear like clouds and then they pass. We know that every transient thing is illusory. Therefore, don't worry about anger. When there's disidentification from the body-mind, these emotions will lessen, until they eventually disappear. They won't be a problem, so, don't make them a problem now!

Q. If I am not the doer and I am not the thinker either, won't the Almighty make me think, moment by moment, which thoughts are necessary for the universal picture? And can't I just let things be on autopilot? You did say Maharaj said that when we are unwell, we should go to the doctor. Can you help reconcile the above two things?

A. I'm amused at how your mind twists things as you attempt to make them fit in accordance with your wishes! You are not the doer and you are not the thinker. At the end stage of the process, all thoughts, all remaining thoughts will be spiritual thoughts that are not troublesome. They will be peaceful, beautiful thoughts - and these will stay.

At the moment, your thoughts are still coming from your conditioning, influences and makeup, in other words, from the mind, ego and intellect. Therefore, these must dissolve, with the help of the Mantra and process. Things can unfold in spontaneous autopilot mode, say, once "you" are out of the picture. But you would not wish to let that happen at present, while the thoughts are coming from identification with the body form. Regarding going to the doctors, if you have a physical problem go and see a doctor. If you have a mental problem, go and see a psychologist because the body-mind problems have nothing to do with your Ultimate Truth, your Ultimate Reality.

Face death head-on

Q. I love the simplicity and the clarity of Maharaj's teachings! They are unequivocal in meaning, unambiguous. They are so clear, leaving no room for compromise. There's no grey areas. For example, I keep this statement close to me at all times to keep me practising continuously and all the way: "Ultimate Reality will not emerge until all body-based knowledge has been removed". I am determined to get rid of fear and wake up well before I am on my deathbed!

A. Yes in this scenario of the last moment of bodily life which is the most testing and challenging moment we face, it is unlikely that with the best will in the world, if the person is lacking Conviction, that he will be able to face the moment without any fear. That is why Maharaj often said to try hard to have the Conviction, well before leaving the body, otherwise you will be shaking and trembling on your death bed. Maharaj advises us not to leave waking up from the dream till the last moment, as it will be impossible to root out all our fears at this testing time.

The fear of death needs to be faced head on because if we have not yet dissolved the illusory ego that carries this weighty concept - of extinction, annihilation, wipe out - before the last moment, then the odds will be stacked against us. Also, the older we are, the more difficult it is to uproot the ingrained concepts.

Having said all that, miracles do happen! If for example, you're close to your Master or Guru and call on them to help you, then assistance will come. The Masters or Gurus are infinitely compassionate. However, to be on the safe side and not leave the door open to unfavourable eventualities, it's better to make sure that Self-Realization has occurred well before your sell-by-date.

Even mentioning the possibility of a miracle can make you complacent and unwilling to carry out the practice. So, please don't take any risks. Make sure this is your last dream, which for many is more like a nightmare than a dream! It is up to you! You have all the tools at your disposal, therefore, use them and set yourself free.

Q. Sometimes during meditation, I feel that I am disappearing. Then I get scared and immediately stop meditating. This has happened a few times. Is this normal?

A. The sensation of disappearance or dissolution, this feeling of death or annihilation can cause fear and panic. Many devotees after practising for some time, experience moments like this. Some devotees, sadly, actually give up at this point because the fear overwhelms them and they can't cope with it. And even though the fear is illusory, it can be very strong. Here, using auto-suggestion such as, "I am not dying, it is only the illusion that is dissolving" and similar statements, can reduce the fear, as well as aid conviction.

Put on your non-dual spectacles

Q. If all is consciousness and this is a dream with actors, then upon the ending of this dream, we will all realize that consciousness is our natural state upon the death of the actor. What then happens to these actors? I can understand that the unawakened would return to the dreams, not as a reincarnation but as another appearance. But I cannot understand what happens to the awakened actor now deceased. Is there an understanding of this?

A. You have a hunger to find out, to know yourself which is very good. You have the bone between your teeth and you won't let it go. That is a great quality for a seeker. You will not give up and are determined to go all the way! So, what happens to the awakened actor after death? You cannot understand what happens after, not really, because it is beyond our understanding. We can guess, imagine, surmise etc., but we cannot know for sure. We can however gain some understanding from the experiences of loved ones who have transitioned, as well as from their partners who have felt the presence of their loved ones around. And we can also know a little from these Masters who have attained *Mahasamadi*.

Throughout history, there have been many indications and fascinating accounts of the hereafter. I remember you asked this question when we first met. I know where it's coming from. You wish to know if your wife, your loved one, will be with you, after leaving the body? Put it this way, stop perceiving yourself as a separate individual and your wife as a separate individual. Put on your nondual spectacles and see her and yourself as formless Oneness. Your essence and her essence are one and the same. We are all part of one Essence, one Energy. As Einstein and others said, energy never dies. It can be transformed into many things, but it will always remain.

When there is awakening within, and say, you drop the body, then your essence, energy continues. The form returns to the formless that you have always been. Putting it another way, Presence becomes Omnipresence. And then your question will be, what kind of activity will this post beingness, enlightened energy have? That we do not know until it happens. But to go back to loved ones, I know from my own experience with my husband, Charles, who left the body in 2018, that his Presence is alive and with me all the time. The love that existed between us continues. It never dies. He's part of me and his Energy or Essence exists eternally, just like mine because it is one and the same. As for the *jnanis*, they are an exceptional species, a little like the *bodhisattvas* of Buddhism. They exist in some plane where they are available to us always. They can appear in a kind of ethereal state, guiding us, protecting us always. I, as well as many others, know this from direct experience. At the moment, in your dream life, you are using the intellect to try and understand. I assure you that through deep meditation, the answers to your questions will appear. Once the mind quietens down and the door is open to Source, the light will shine and pave the way for all the answers to appear to your questions. Then you will know from direct experience. Guaranteed! Meanwhile keep meditating, hammering, persevering.

You are unborn

Q. Maharaj says that there is no birth and no death, that everything is an appearance, a projection of Selfless Self. Does this mean that I will never see my loved ones again when I pass away?

A. There is no separate "I". You are not separate from your loved ones. There is only one, not two. There is no duality which means that your loved ones are already a part of you, a part of that same Essence that exists as only one Essence. You will not see them in the literal sense because there is no "you" and no "they", but the love will be there in that Oneness.

Q. Even though I don't perceive myself as a body, I am aware that I still have the deepest fear of dying. It keeps me from complete detachment which I feel is something necessary to progress. To fight fear, I often do something that frightens me, however, it does not seem to work. Recently, I've experienced something that I call "show love to the fear" as a solution.

A. There is no birth and there is no death. You are unborn. The fear is coming from the pseudo ego, who you think you are, i.e., the mind-body complex. You are not that! In order to liberate from the small self, you need to absorb the knowledge of your true nature and grow in the conviction that you were not the body, that you are not the body and never were.

Recognize that this life is a long dream and that you are the witness, even beyond the witness. The Mantra helps us to dissolve the ego and the illusory layers that have covered over our Presence, our Reality - that one Essence in which we all share. We are not separate beings, but part of the one Omnipresent Reality.

I think you will benefit from reading a very simple presentation of Nonduality in the book, *Who am I?* It covers the concept of fear, among other obstacles that are in the way of us seeing clearly and realizing our true nature. At the end of the bodily life, everything dissolves. For Conviction, we need to erase the ego, quieten the mind, let the mind drop back into Source. Use the Mantra to keep hammering yourself. As long as fear is still around, it means you don't have the Conviction that you are That, that you are beyond the body mind, that you are eternal, omnipresent, that you are the Presence behind everything. It is easy to read, however, absorbing the knowledge takes more time.

Suffering

Q. I notice it will take more time. It sinks in, little by little. Conceptually I understand, but emotionally if someone close to me is suffering or close to death, then immediately the fear comes.

A. Who is suffering? You are still viewing yourself as a separate entity and someone else as a separate entity. Suffering is caused by identification with the body-form. You are not that. Fear is an illusion, like other emotions and thoughts – they are not real. But we have been brought up with them and they have become part of our illusory make-up. We have been conditioned to protect ourselves and feel fear, believing ourselves to be separate selves, when we are not that at all.

There is only Oneness, one Presence and we are all a part of that. It is the power or energy behind the body-mind that enables it to function. Be assured that the fear is something that will reduce with your practice because when you realize that there is no you, then there will not be any fear. But first of all, you need the Conviction that there is no you, that you don't exist. All that exists is one Reality. And when you are more in touch with that,

Ultimate Reality will begin to emerge because you are beginning to dissolve. And when that happens, the fear will dissolve. And then, little by little, everything will fall away.

When you know you are eternal, what is there to fear? There is no death and no birth. You need more convincing. The knowledge has to go from the head to the heart, so that the core of your being accepts it. Maharaj used to say that it is very easy for the uneducated, illiterate devotees because when the Master tells them they are Ultimate Truth, the devotees accept it, without thinking, without question, without counter-arguments. The fear you speak of will disappear when the knowledge is fully accepted and absorbed - when you know that you are not this entity. It has already started to happen. Just continue with your practice and be patient.

Q. I feel I am going through an inner war, with endless thoughts and horrible memories surfacing from the past! I am also quite disturbed by the war that is going on with the Israelis and Palestinians. I can't bear to see so much suffering. I'm hoping that the journey back to the Self will be quick. Also, I am wondering what my responsibility is as the holder of consciousness? Do spontaneous happenings mean no responsibility and just witnessing? The suffering is very present. Much love and longing for sanity. Time is short and the urge to return to Reality is present.

A. Try and use the Mantra more to counter the memories as they arise. Don't let them linger and try not to give them your attention. You are not back at the starting point. All this is a dream, an illusion. It may not help to hear this, but it is a fact. The inner wars and the outer wars are both illusions. When Nisargadatta Maharaj was asked about Hitler and the pain and suffering that he caused, his reply was the same: "All of it is illusion! Nothing is happening!" Your responsibility is to continue to behave as before, with kindness and compassion. You know that life is a dream. Witness the goings-on and at the same time, help others and be compassionate towards them. As you know, suffering comes from your identification with the body-form. Keep reminding yourself that you are not that. At the same time, it can be very challenging to view the horrors you speak of.

I am praying for you to have ongoing courage, for you not to be terribly affected by what you see. Stay with the Seer, not with the seen! Know that Maharaj is with you always, as I am too. Know that this, too, will pass. It is good that the urge to touch base with reality is strong. The sooner, the better. The *bhajans* will keep you uplifted. Also, we had a beautiful celebration last week for Shri Siddharameshwar's *Punyatithi*, "Death" Anniversary). I will send you the link. It will inspire you! Meanwhile take great care. Much love and blessings.

What you are in Reality
has never undergone any suffering

Q. The way I see it is that suffering is a call to Self-enquiry, to investigation. And thanks to the bodily sufferings, I have understood that I am nothing.

A. Who suffers? Suffering only happens because of your identification with the body-mind. You are not the body nor the mind, nor your fears, nor your pain. You are unborn. When you have the conviction that you are not the body, not the mind, not anything that is temporary, then you're entering the path of reality, instead of illusion. While suffering can be a great teacher, once you have learned from it, there is no further need. There was no suffering prior to being. You say you have understood that you are nothing, but what you have missed is that you are also everything. You are Presence, Energy, the Source, the Power behind everything.

When we remove the illusory layers with the help of the Mantra, you will begin to return to the Source that you are - your natural state, your permanent state. What you are in Reality has never undergone any suffering. It has never been touched by anything and remains pure and pristine. That Presence is the power behind everything. The workings of the mind that lift you one minute and bring you down the next is part of the illusory dream called life. Happiness and unhappiness, all the different kinds of moods that we experience, pass. All that passes is illusion. When all the superimpositions, the conditioning, the brainwashing, etc., has been undone, when the clouds have all gone, then the light will emerge once more.

Experiences are Illusory

Q. I really miss some kind of at least onetime experience which would indicate that I am on the right track because I'm starting to have doubts. Not doubts about the teachings or the knowledge or faith, but doubts about the relative correctness of my *sadhana*. There are thoughts that I'm technically performing meditation and other disciplines incorrectly and that my involvement is not enough... therefore, there are no results and experiences. Yet, I understand that a year is not so much. But then again, it's not just one day or a month either.

I've been conscientiously doing daily meditation and *bhajans* all this time, regardless of the circumstances and yet, still, I don't see any obvious changes, either on the mental level or any other. Let's say, in your case, you describe in *Timeless Years* that you had various experiences that encouraged you and deepened your Conviction. In my case. it feels like I'm knocking on a closed door.

A. Back to the "I", back to the ego again. "I" really miss some kind of one-time experience. Recognize that the mind is playing games. You say you want experiences to indicate that you're on the right track. Leave that to me! That is my job. Everyone is different! Some have experiences, some not. Some have many, while others have none. It is not important! This is another mind game attempting to weaken your *sadhana*. Ignore this thought!

The truth is that, at times, you probably find the practice dull, dry and boring. The ego is looking for a show of lights and fireworks to alleviate the monotony of the predictable. Results will show, not through experiences but in the way you live, act, react and respond to different situations. The ego says: "I understand a year is not much". If you really understand the teachings and have absorbed them, then you would know better than to count the years! Time is a concept – again, another mind-game.

Q. I have never felt peace like this, but at the same time, I feel giddy and restless, like I want to tell you everything that I am experiencing. This is subtle ego perhaps wanting your approval. I would love to connect over skype sometime soon.

A. Sounds like a great adventure. It is not subtle ego or seeking approval. It is all happening spontaneously and there is joy, excitement and freshness. So, of course, your wish to share is only natural and I'm looking forward to hearing all about what is not happening. Until then, have fun!

Interest in the dreamworld

Q. I've dropped some time-consuming habits to make more time for the practice, or as Maharaj says, to "spend time with you". The Mantra is happening, Self-enquiry is happening and meditation, too, though not at rigorously structured times. There is a pull towards learning the *bhajans* and devotion is natural and spontaneous. So, it is happening, but not regimented. Is this being too cavalier and not serious enough?

A. Good start! Dropping some habits in favour of the practice is not easy, so, well done! The discipline will come and you will fall into a regular pattern of practice three times a day, or when you can. It is a big improvement from indulging in worldly entertainment.

Mantra, Self-enquiry and meditation are taking place, plus you say you're drawn towards learning the *bhajans* and this is not just a thought that you should do it, but a divine pull. That is excellent! The seed has been planted and best of all, you report that devotion is natural and spontaneous. This means your heart is opening up to the knowledge and the guidance of the Masters.

You ask if you're not serious enough about the practice? I would say that compared to giving your attention to worldly affairs and enjoying the "seen", there has been a definite shift to stay with the "Seer" and involve yourself in the practice. All very encouraging! Go slowly in the beginning or the ego will rebel! Steady is good! Keep on doing what you're doing. Well done!

Attachments

Q. I still have a deep desire for intimacy. It is hard to ignore. You, like Maharaj, do not give credence to these materialistic things which will fade away and lose significance in the practice of the Mantra, right? But I need to ask you: Should I look for a relationship or just throw myself into the practice more deeply? You have not replied to my last few questions. Is everything alright?

A. When you understand that everything is illusion, then why are you still running after, eg., the illusory form of a woman. You are not the body, but Presence. Without Presence, all bodies are dead! So, why not keep your focus on the energy that powers everything, instead of its shadow or reflection! You sound as though you prefer to have a few minutes ecstasy, instead of permanent ecstatic peace and joy! It is such a waste of your energy to keep clinging to desires, women etc., all of it just a show, instead of That which never changes.

Sometimes I don't reply to you because you are not listening to the guidance. In spite of it, you keep repeating the same things, over and over. You know these illusions are fading and yet you still try to hold onto them which prevents the practice from going deeper. Take the practice seriously! There is no need to keep going over old ground! Be serious! Don't waste any more time feeding your imagination!

Q. The more I go deeper into the practice, the more time I want to spend alone. But my wife is not keen that I am spending so much time in meditation. She wants more of my attention. She is naturally attached to me, but I am quickly losing interest in some of the things we used to do together, even the stuff we used to talk about. She wants me to watch TV with her every night and when I do, I can't stop thinking that I'm wasting my time, that I could be meditating instead. Is this a normal occurrence of the practice. I mean drifting away from one's partner? I don't want to lose her.

A. It is a good sign that you wish to spend more time alone to meditate more. Even at this early stage, something is stirring within you, spontaneously, and you recognize its importance. You are being driven by your desire to know yourself, to know your Reality. It is natural for you to become more detached and less interested in worldly things. Just explain to your wife how important your practice is to you. The wish to spend time alone does not mean you're drifting away from her, it means you're searching for truth. But be moderate! Why not sometimes appear as if you're watching TV, but recite the Mantra at the same time?

Don't impose spirituality on anyone!

Q. My husband loves me very much but he has no interest in spirituality. I would like to share it with him because it is the most important thing in my life, but what chance do I have when he thinks it is all nonsense! Therefore, I have to do my practice in secret, when he's not there.

A. Don't impose spirituality on anyone if they are not interested! If your husband is not interested, then don't try and take him along with you. But at the same time, pay no attention to what he thinks. Don't listen to his thoughts or opinions about it and just quietly continue with your practice. You are doing it for you. Don't be discouraged!

Q. I know *Brahman* will never allow it, but somehow, like a moth is attracted to a flame, my desire to meet a woman persists.

A. If everything and everyone is illusion, then why keep running after illusion, instead of uncovering the Reality within you. 'Man' and 'woman' are illusory concepts related to the body form and not what we are in essence. When you are younger there are bodily needs and desires and you fulfil them, but when you are older you should be turning within because you know you are not the body form.

Q. Could you share some words of advice regarding the dream state and the fear of death? I would be blessed if you do!

A. There is no birth and there is no death. You are unborn. Fear is an illusion! The fear is coming from the pseudo ego, from who you think you are - ie the mind-body complex you are attached to. You are not that! In order to be liberated from the small self and its associated fears, what is needed is for you to absorb the knowledge of your true nature and grow in the Conviction that you are not the body and never were.

When the pseudo self dissolves, the ghost of fear will also vanish! Recognize that this life is a long dream. You are the witness and even beyond the witness. The Mantra helps us to dissolve the ego and the illusory layers that have covered over our Presence, our Reality - that One Essence in which we all share. We are not separate beings but part of the one, omnipresent Reality.

If all is a dream, why bother?

Q. I have a doubt. As per Advaita Vedanta, all that I see including my own body is a dream, my dream. After 60 I don't have a source of income. So, if I start a business, all my clients will be dream-clients of this dream body. It seems better to rather trust to God or destiny for my food and survival?

A. Currently, all that you see is also a dream and your colleagues at work are dream colleagues, therefore, the dream just continues! As Maharaj used to say, we need to work, do something to earn a living, otherwise we are beggars. Know that you are always looked after, however, you must play your part too. You cannot expect financial assistance to drop from the sky into your lap. So, you should explore how to make enough money to survive!

Q. Would you speak about why you chose an image of looking in a mirror for the cover of the *Who am I?* book?

A. As we look at the mirror, we're looking at ourselves and asking the question, "Who am I?" And if you notice, at the end of the book there is the same picture without any reflection and without the question mark. This symbolizes that after the journey, there is nothing there. That's basically what it's about.

Q. Would you elaborate on the dedication to Ramakant Maharaj in the book? You do not thank Maharaj for teaching you everything you know?

A. I say "To my Beloved Maharaj who taught me everything I don't know". If I had said "who taught me everything I know", that would mean there is the illusion of an "I", as well as the knowledge, when we know we are beyond knowledge. There was no knowledge prior to being, therefore, I say, "who taught me everything I don't know". This means that I know that I don't know. I know I am formless as I was prior to being, without an "I", without knowledge. We are prior to and beyond knowledge. We say "I don't know" because everything is a dream, an illusion. No knowledge is knowledge.

Process

Q. What is the process we need to undergo? It seems like a solitary one, tinged with anxiety?

A. The book, *Selfless Self* explains the three stages of the process, namely Self-enquiry, Self-knowledge and Self-Realization. Also, listening to, or singing the *bhajans* will help you absorb the knowledge, so that it does not remain as dry, intellectual knowledge. There should not be any anxiety. Who is anxious and why? You are not left alone on the journey either. Know that the Masters are blessing you and showering you with grace and helping you go forward and deeper. There should be eagerness and determination en route. One day, Spontaneous Conviction will arise and then there will not be any further need for practice. Just devotion/*puja* to the Masters, to thank them for enabling our liberation from the ego. Continued devotion will keep us humble.

Q. Maharaj says, initially, you have to undergo the process of meditation, *bhajans*, etc., till Spontaneous Conviction. "Initially" seems to suggest a small period, early on. Can you stick your neck out and say what is the average period you have generally observed? Can you venture a guess for me? Can you tell what you have seen is the average time for serious seekers to finish the preprocessing, one may say, before the inner spirit drives it on autopilot?

A. What does "initially" mean? It depends on several things: spiritual maturity, dedication and commitment. The length of time can vary from weeks or months to longer periods. Have faith in what Maharaj says, i.e. if you follow the instructions, Self-Realization will ensue. Ultimately, it is up to you as to how disciplined and serious you are about the practice and how important you view the end goal. And in your case, taking control of the doubts and not giving them any power to hold back your progress!

Practice

Q. Is there a need to artificially create the realized state? For example, during the day, imagine that you see yourself in other people and the world around? You feel the space in yourself and not yourself in the space, etc?

A. Don't try to feel anything! During the day, keep doing *japa*, as well as convincing yourself, using short statements such as, "I am unborn". "I am not the body". "Everything is illusion". Don't use the mind to artificially manufacture the realized state. We are trying to weaken the mind. Don't use your imagination!

These questions arise because you do not have a firm knowledge background or solid foundation. First step, you need to absorb the basic knowledge: "That you are not the body. That everything is an illusion. That you are unborn. That you are prior to being. That this is a dream. That you are an actor playing a role. That nothing is real". You need to hammer yourself with these statements, so that we can undo the brainwashing and conditioning. Do it with joy in your heart and a skip in your step! As Maharaj says, this is happy knowledge! It should not be seen as work or duty, but should give you the drive and determination to "go for it" and be free.

Freedom from your little self is near. It is in your hands. You have all the tools at your disposal, therefore, go deep within to know yourself with drive and passion. The foundation, your foundation, should be there. There is nothing except Selfless Self. To build on that foundation, you should be contemplating on the knowledge and accepting it, more and more deeply.

The process is not about belief. We don't have to believe in anything but when the Master says something, when He tells you the truth, all we need do is accept it, and that's precisely what we have great difficulty in doing. Instead of analyzing, "what does he mean by this?" or "what does he mean by that?" or breaking down all that the Master says, all you need do is accept them as truth, with the help of the Mantra, Self-enquiry and applying the knowledge. Gradually, you will be able to live the knowledge, be the knowledge thus bridging the gap between beingness and knowingness.

Q. Another recent thought/feeling I have begun to have is that I am not the one who performs the practice and tries to achieve enlightenment, that the ego is the seeker. In the book, *Be With You,* there is a quote where Ramakant Maharaj says that the seeker is the Ultimate Truth. So, after all, is the Ultimate Truth the seeker or is the Ultimate Truth observing or witnessing the seeker?

A. As I said, the foundation your foundation, should be "I am Ultimate Reality". There is only one, not two. The mind separates this Oneness and calls everything by names, by many different names. When the Conviction is there: "I am Ultimate Reality", there will be no questions. We have to use language for worldly existence because we are in the body form where we try to give meanings to the words. For example, the "seeker", the "witness", etc. If everything is Ultimate

Reality, then it follows that there is no such thing as a seeker or witness, or words like Ultimate Reality, for that matter. Everything is illusion: you, the mind, ego, concepts, feelings, layers of conditioning. These concepts have to be dissolved as they are covering up your Ultimate Reality, like clouds obscuring the sun. You are Ultimate Reality full stop, manifesting as a somebody because you have forgotten your identity.

When you start seeking after truth, when you ask the question: "Is the seeker the ego or ultimate truth?", that is the mind dividing the one Reality again. Everything is illusion. You are unborn, so, why analyze the unborn child? There is nothing to say. Ultimate Reality plays the role of the seeker. To understand the process, let's break it down: There is only Ultimate Truth. You are That. You are what you are seeking.

Ultimate Truth is indescribable. But let's say it is the Essence, the Power, the Presence behind everything. Follow this logically and it will lead to the Conviction that behind the illusory seeker, there is only Ultimate Truth. And, therefore, the seeker is Ultimate Truth. When you ask, is the seeker the ego or Ultimate Truth, this is just the mind playing tricks on you, and importantly, what this shows, is that you do not have a solid base yet. The truth is not established in you, at all times, permanently. The Conviction is not there! You are beyond words and worlds. There is no seeker and no witness. These are just words. You're taking the words for real and they are not. Where was the seeker, the witness, prior to beingness?

One further point which I have elucidated in *Who Am I?* about the process: Teachers of Advaita Vedanta will take students through the process, like I am taking you. First you hear the Truth of your Reality: You are Ultimate Truth. Then you undergo the process of *neti neti*, discarding everything as illusion - What is reality? What is illusion? Using discrimination and separating what you are not, from what you are. Finally, you are told and realize for yourself, that everything is *Brahman* or Ultimate Truth.

After a shift in perspective, there is the realization that the world is the projection of your Spontaneous Presence. This means that everything is a play, a reflection of that one Ultimate Reality. There must be the Conviction that you are established in Ultimate Reality. You must know deep down that this is your base, your Source. It has always been because you are prior to beingness. That Ultimate Reality is your eternal reality. When this truth of your reality is established within you, you will not be led astray by these intellectual questions. You end the first question asking, "so, after all, is the Ultimate Truth the seeker or the witness?" The answer is yes, yes! But again, Ultimate Reality is beyond the witness, the Seer, the Knower. You are beyond everything you can put into words. It is necessary to let go of everything you have accumulated since childhood: identity, attachments, roles, property etc.

You are not a monk

Q. Logically it's all clear, but at the same time, you say that we do not need to neglect our obligations, not to quit our job, family, etc. And on the other hand, we need to give up all this. It turns out like a stick with two ends, either I need to make a choice and give up everything by stepping aside, or continue to stay in all this illusion and continue to play by my rules. I'm not comparing but trying to figure it out.

A. And I say again, you're using the mind and taking the teachings literally. You need to establish the knowledge of your Reality deeper within you. You have not absorbed the knowledge yet. You are attached to who you are: likes and dislikes, conditioning, values, family, children, behaviour, etc. Our goal is to loosen these attachments. Yes, we need to carry out our duties, work, family etc. There is no either/or, as you say, or a stick with two ends. You conclude that either you need to make a choice, step aside or continue to cook in the illusory sauce. The block here is the "I" who thinks it has to make a choice. You should know by now that there is no "I", that this "I" is incapable of making choices anyhow. This "I" is just a big illusion that keeps tripping you up.

Letting go or giving up is an internal act, an internal process that unfolds from the practice and the deepening of the knowledge. If the Conviction of "I am Ultimate Reality" is there, then your attention would be fixed on that alone, at all times, and not on the mind, trying to work out the either/or scenario.

We are able to loosen the attachments and continue to role play because of the firm Conviction of our Reality. There is no conflict. Nisargadatta Maharaj and Ramakant Maharaj were both part of a householder lineage. They did their practice in the midst of family life! You are not a monk! No need to retreat in a cave! No need to escape at all. What are you escaping from when you know that everything is illusion?

Q. When thoughts come and I identify them as some kind of unreasonableness or mental garbage, do I need to discard them as unnecessary? Do I need to try to switch to the one who perceives these thoughts - let's call him a witness of thoughts? But at the same time, there is some kind of resistance or rejection. Is it necessary to simply observe the thought, regardless of whether it's reasonable or unreasonable, without conducting any analysis and discrimination, just knowing that it is just an illusory thought? Just to know that I am not the thought, that it is separate from me, regardless of whether it is good or bad?

A. During meditation, when thoughts arise, all you need do is ignore the thoughts and keep reciting the Mantra. Always bring your attention back to reciting the Mantra. When your attention strays, there is no point in analyzing illusion. As I said before, only give recurrent thoughts attention. Sometimes, there are deep-seated issues that keep arising. The same ones keep coming up and up, again and again. If that happens, it's a sign that you need to give these issues attention using Self-enquiry. But do not break up the meditation. Carry out further investigation outside of your allocated, meditation time.

Q. All of us are doing the practice. Everyone is involved in different ways. Everyone is repeating the Mantra as much as possible, meditating and being with oneself, with Selfless Self, concentrating on the Concentrator, etc. But nevertheless, every day to some extent or other, we are again involved in illusion, doing our work, doing business, communicating with people, returning again and again, to old, destructive habits etc. It turns out that through practice we purify ourselves, get rid of illusion, but when we again get involved in illusion, we get polluted, clogged, and it is like a kind of tug-of war.

At some point over time, as we continue to do the practice, such distractions and involvements in illusion become less and less. Purification happens more and more and at some point, the tight rope is on our side and Spontaneous Conviction comes. Or, is it not so?

A. If you practice regularly then the layers of Illusion will gradually dissolve. You may not be aware of any changes taking place, but they are taking place. In time, you will notice that you are not dragged into the illusion as much, but instead, more able to remain as the Witness. Keep up the practice and the Conviction will follow.

You are not the doer

Q. In *Selfless Self*, Shri Ramakant Maharaj talks about not neglecting family members, family life, etc., otherwise it will become selfish spirituality. Okay I admit that I have shifted a lot of responsibilities to my wife. She's constantly tired, gets stressed, depressed. On that basis, constantly, when my help and involvement are needed, I am in my room, doing my practice, meditation, *bhajans*, meetings, etc. No matter what happens, I always continue my practice with the thought that I don't care about anything. Plus, when there are some dramas, problems and different situations with the children, I convince myself that nothing is really happening, that it is all an illusion, a distraction from reality. I try not to get involved and not give it any serious importance. This way, I am not distracted. Whereas if I dedicate time to my family, the children, I will have no time for meditation and *bhajans*, etc. What to do about it all?

A. There's a lot of "I, I, I's" here in your question. Remember that while you're attending to your work, practice or other activity, you are not the doer. If you think you are, it will drain and stress you and that sounds like what's been happening. Let Selfless Self attend to everything while you stay as the Witness.

In Nisargadatta's radar

Q. I wanted to tell you that although I have not been able to attend the meetings, I'm still very much on the practice and have lots of things to share. I'm especially a bit sad that I could not attend Ramakant Maharaj's birthday, since he has done so much for me. I was working that day. There have been lots of interesting developments.

My inner teacher seems to be strengthening, or at least, I seem to be able to listen to him more clearly. Sometimes he sends me clear messages through dreams or unlikely synchronicities. Something very strange that I've been noticing is that people around me seem to be growing a lot more sensitive to my thoughts, almost like a kind of telepathy. I've also had some dreams with the Masters. One of the more remarkable ones was with Nisargadatta Maharaj. I had an appointment with him and I was really scared because I knew he was a very strict Master, but when he saw me, he was actually very supportive and encouraged me greatly. It was a very wholesome dream. I've also seen the face of Ramakant Maharaj while meditating.

I feel the presence of the lineage and my inner Master everywhere I go. I feel like they might also be helping my family economically too. Oddly enough, just today my mother entered my room, shedding tears of joy because her loan had been forgiven. And when she hugged me, I ended up in such a position that I faced the smiling pictures of the Masters which spontaneously filled me with gratitude.

A. It's a nice story. What you relate in your email is really good and great that the Masters are with you in your waking and dream states. You are blessed. Nisargadatta appearing as very strict is only a veneer to get people to wake up. I'm glad he was gentle with you and encouraging. That's a lovely story about your mother's loan cancellation. It is true that the Masters look after us in all ways. When you are in their radar they will help you, as and when, needed. The compassion of the Masters has no bounds. Beautiful! We should meet online soon to catch up more.

The act of bowing deflates the ego

Q. Namaste I'm going on my retreat shortly. In the meantime, I've been reading from *Selfless Self* every day, watching videos of Maharaj, videos of the *bhajans*, etc. I have had some experiences that I think may be significant, but only as signs of progress and not the truth itself.

First, I was watching a video in which Maharaj gives advice about negative thoughts. His message, as you know, is to simply reject those thoughts that diminish us, gets us into quarrels, make us agitated, etc. I don't know why, but that night, I was able to do this with my own, frequently depressive thoughts, as they arose. I gently, but assertively, said "no" to the ones I didn't like and it worked immediately. Suddenly, it was as if I had been submerged in a dirty swamp full of mud and finally rose to the surface. Previously, I believed my thoughts had power of their own, the power to pull me back under, but that night I proved to myself that I could simply decline. They were completely dependent on my accepting them all along. I laughed and cried and bowed down to the floor before the image of Maharaj on the screen in the deepest relief, deepest gratitude for he showed me a power I never knew I had.

Lately, while reading from *Selfless Self*, especially the parts in capital letters, I often spontaneously feel a surge of electricity or Pure Energy running through me. Sometimes it's so powerful that I double over, not in pain, but in surging bliss. This has been happening more and more frequently. In the Kriya Yoga tradition, we pay close attention to the body, especially the spine, trying to induce the same current of ecstatic buzzing energy, by breathing slowly, going through the chakras, etc., but Maharaj's words by themselves have the same effect.

A. It all sounds really wonderful! You are already becoming aware of your power and experiencing this directly: that you are not a slave of your thoughts and feelings as they arise. That you can choose which ones to accept and which ones to reject. This is very encouraging and I am so happy this experience brought you to your knees to express gratitude to Maharaj. Giving thanks to the Master is an integral part of the process. Each time you bow, the ego is deflated more and more.

Q. How helpful is it to dissolve the fundamental concept, the illusion of being a separate entity?

A. In answer to your question, not only does it help, but it is absolutely essential. We are already realized, already our true nature, but that is obscured by layers of illusion, by the false "I" and all its creations. We need to remove everything that is obscuring our true nature. Self-realization means freedom or liberation from the small "I", the small self. The small, illusory "I" cannot coexist with Ultimate Reality which is what you are, therefore, we need to demolish everything we think we are. All the constructs, the layers, impositions, etc.

Gripped by a fever

Q. I have no interest in my work or prestige. If I could leave my job, I would leave it tomorrow. Relations with my wife are strained, to say the least. My only interest now is in Self-Realization.

A. It is not really my place to comment on your life situation, as it is a worldly issue that is separate from spirituality and therefore, has nothing to do with it. All I would say is don't make any impulsive decisions! Having said that, I understand totally the disinterest in work matters, prestige, wife, etc., that you have felt which continues to impact you.

Your life situation stated in positive terms, I can relate to wholeheartedly. Nothing is more important in this life than Self-realization. And when we are gripped by this fever which we can sometimes call madness, sometimes everything else pales into insignificance. However, to counter what I have just said, the lineage is a householder lineage. All the Masters were able to attend to their practice, while attending to their work and family life as well.

Q. In one sense I am doing this *sadhana* because I am unhappy and feel lacking something, and this *sadhana* will help realise the divinity, or rather help unrealise whatever is hiding that divinity. On the other hand, wouldn't it be easier if I were to drop everything, since what does it matter if I come out of this dream or not? Why not leave it to *Brahman* and resign myself completely to him. But ha ha, wait, the fact is I am not able to surrender. I have this ego which does not want to surrender, so the lineage path is to bring out clarity out of the whole mess that our ego perennially takes pleasure in putting us in, right Ann? What stops us from surrendering completely? Can anything be done to remove the obstacles to surrender?

A. Your assessment is right. And you just need to continue the practice. Now you can see how much resistance there is!! Continue the practice till the "I" has gone and all that is left is the Light that you are! You have apparently been using this method of Self-enquiry for a lifetime and where has it got you? It needs to work, otherwise, why continue it as a habit only?

The process is not meant to be a comfortable ride

Q. You are right. It's just that the mantra recitation does not, on a moment-by-moment level, give me peace. I have to accept it as a detoxification exercise. No instant gratification! Is that right?

A. You are undergoing a clearing out process that brings everything to the surface. It is not meant to be a comfortable ride. The peace will come. You already have had a taste, so, be patient. Don't accept all these negative thoughts. The best way forward is to ignore them! The practice is all about concentration and giving your attention to the Mantra. When you direct your attention to the nonsense going on in the mind and give it importance which it never deserves, you keep falling backwards.

Q. Truth is the *sadhana* and the Guru's presence in my life is what is making me tolerate life and spurring me on to continue living. There's hardly anything else left!

A. The Conviction is growing. When you say "there's hardly anything else left", that is very positive because what is left is all an illusion! What is spurring you on spiritually is, or should be, knowing that the practice will bear fruit, so that who you truly are will be revealed. Then the bliss will flow!

Q. Since the last occurrence of resistance and your blessing, the resistance to the Mantra has reduced and it is almost reaching back to incessant chanting. I will maintain the momentum. Further, the Mantra seems to have added some teeth to my personality. Also, that my professional mode of working seems to have been strengthened. The Mantra seems to touch all aspects of life. But for me the most touching thing is that I have a

Godmother who will be there for me till eternity. I am in safe hands.

A. Very happy to hear. Yes, it is true that efficiency and confidence rise. And both inner and outer changes take place.

Don't see Self-Realization as a personal investment

Q. I have been devoted to the practice now for two years. I have sacrificed a lot of time and family life for meditation. And still there is no end result. Sometimes I doubt that what I desire most in life, Self-Realization, is going to happen?

A. You are looking at the goal of Self-Realization as a personal investment. It should not be seen in this way. The ego is still very much there. And likewise, there should not be any desires left. Your outlook or perspective is ego-centred. You want to see results on your terms. Self-Realization means liberation from that small "I" who believes it is sacrificing, desiring and grasping. Who wants liberation? You know that time is a concept so why are you counting the years? Two years is nothing in the context of a lifetime lived as the pseudo self. You cannot keep one foot in illusion and one in Reality. Self-surrender by abandoning all illusion, hopes and wishes. Continue the practice without expectations, time limits, desires. Remove these barriers! Be humble and patient!

Feels good for whom?

Q. I guess the gist of any spiritual practice as emphasised by Maharaj and you is that what matters is what works and not what just feels good?

A. Of course! What feels good is body-based. Feels good for whom? Hammering, chiselling, excavating the ego and all the attachments will certainly not feel good!

Q. I know I should be reciting incessantly. Sometimes there is silence but then a burst of mental activity, doubts, questions follow.

A. There needs to be more alertness, so that you do not give this intellectual chatter your attention. You should be able to catch the thoughts before they catch you and ignore them as they arise, instead of feeding them with attention.

Q. Life continues with its difficulties, but thanks to your blessings, the Mantra chanting is continuing, albeit not so vigorously, but intermittently at all times.

A. Very happy to hear that! When Ultimate Truth is unwaveringly established, the question of whether your life is going right or not will no longer arise or be an issue at all because "you" will not be there to comment on the status of the illusory life.

Q. Do I try to remain still, and then, when disturbed by thoughts, ask, "where was this thought prior to beingness?" Or (example when I am overtly disturbed and assailed by thoughts), pre-empt the process by cutting the thought at its very root (even before it sprouts), by repeatedly asking, where was this thought prior to beingness?

A. Cut it at its roots! You don't want it to sprout. Be alert and keep up the practice.

Q. And when the thought has been cut, we remain in silence, the state prior to being, our natural state of *Brahman*, is that it? And remain therein until disturbed by thoughts, once more? Secondly, do you suggest a fixed time every day for meditation, or interspersed with meditation or round the clock, except where the mind is needed for work?

A. Arrest the thought and return to centre, to reality. At this stage of your practice, forget about remaining in silence! The practice is about training yourself NOT to fall into illusion. In other words, prevent the thoughts from taking you on a merry go round. A fixed time for hammering with the Mantra is good and then *Japa* throughout the day... endeavouring to stay with reality as much as possible.

Q. When I was in your company and after Initiation, I felt so strong and prepared to face anything, ready to battle all the illusion that came my way. But now that I am back home, and back to work, I have fallen into old habits and ways. I feel disillusioned.

A. You cannot expect everything to change overnight. Old habits don't just vanish, they need to be replaced with new habits, like regular meditation and devotion. The Mantra is not a magic wand. It is a powerful tool that will bring steady results with your efforts. Don't be so easily disillusioned. Approach the task in hand with maturity and common sense. You cannot eliminate a whole lifetime in a few days. You have the necessary tools to hammer the ego and slowly emerge from this illusory world. So, now, with renewed vigour restart your daily practice. All is well. And remember, that you are not alone. The Master's blessings are always with you!

Best not to ask "Am I close to the end?"

Q. There is largely, say, 90%, an unperturbed feeling towards everything. Am I close to the end?

A. Indifference is a good sign but it is only one sign. Your impatience is often transparent in your messages. Be patient! It was only a few days ago that you had fallen big time into illusion, without even being aware of it. Best not to ask "Am I close to the end?" Keep hammering that "I".

Q. When my meditation practice is not going well because I am unable to concentrate, I feel frustrated and guilty. Then more negative feelings come up along with thoughts like: "Self-Realization is never going to happen to me", which makes me feel even worse and depressed.

A. I have told you before to ignore the negative feelings and thoughts. Why are you still believing in them? Why are you giving them any attention? Everyone experiences days similar to yours, when they are unable to concentrate. Don't hold on to the negatives! Don't dwell on them. Let it go! It is just a blip! You have heard the Good News! So, be happy! I remember Maharaj used to say to visitors who used to whine: "Why the long faces! The knowledge I have shared is happy knowledge!" Therefore, instead of falling into depression when the practice does not go smoothly, read a paragraph from *Selfless Self* or *Ultimate Truth* instead, which will instantly change your mood. Be happy!

Maya has no power

Q. As hard as I try, I feel that *Maya* has so much power that she always wins. Sometimes I feel as if I have made progress, and then, suddenly I realize I've fallen again and worse still, I've not even been aware of it for a whole day. What am I doing wrong?

A. Don't try so hard and don't be so hard on yourself! Be kind to yourself and approach the practice with a light heart, not a heavy mood. *Maya* has no power because it is complete and utter illusion. The only power *maya* has is what you have given it. It is early days in the process of dismantling and removing all the layers of illusion that you accumulated throughout your life. When the knowledge of Reality, your Reality, is absorbed more deeply, the power that you imagine *maya* has will crumble and eventually disappear. But for now, be patient. You cannot expect to rid yourself of illusion in a couple of months. But what you can do is to stop objectifying *maya* and perceiving it as a powerful force. I reiterate that it has no power. There is only one power, one Source, one Reality. You are That!

Impatient for Self-Realization

Q. I am impatient for Self-Realization. I have high expectations of what it will be like for me. I cannot wait for the changes to take place and all the new things that will come my way.

A. There's a lot of "I's" "my's" and "me's", here. All this kind of talk is creating obstacles for Self-Realization. You need to keep hammering this "I", the ego or pseudo self, until it is silenced completely. And be under no delusion that such high expectations will be fulfilled, nor that any new thing will come your way!

Put simply, Self-Realization means That which remains after removing all the intellectual, psychological and emotional layers of baggage. Everything is already inbuilt within you. You are the source of happiness, peace and love, so don't expect anything new to be added. You are already complete and whole.

These teachings are not leading you to something new. All that is happening is that you are being guided to undo and remove the layers of illusion, so that your inner fire, which has been lying dormant, can re-ignite. Keep hammering! Undo everything you have learned which has conditioned you! You will not be able to know who you are unless the imagined you, the pseudo entity has been cleared out, removed, and swept away.

Q. If everything is already within me, then why do I need to do any practice?

A. We need a practice in order to remember our true identity, our original nature which we have forgotten. We were all programmed to find meaning, happiness, peace and love in the wrong places. Instead of looking inwards, we focussed outwards in search of self-fulfilment. We became addicted to the world, to others, to "the seen". The appearance of the phenomenal world sucked us in, distracting us from the fundamental goal of getting to know who we truly are. This practice or process is a cleansing one that will remove everything.

The secret of your existence is already within you, buried under a mound of imaginary concepts such as self-image, ideas, beliefs, status, roles, accomplishments, etc. You need to undo everything you have learned, which has conditioned you because you will not be able to know who you are unless the imagined you, the pseudo entity has been cleared out and swept away.

You are Ultimate Reality, Ultimate Truth which means that you do not lack anything. Nothing needs to be added to you because you already have the whole package. You are already whole. Your original nature is formless, without add-ons. However, to know this deep down and return home to your Source, your place of origin, deconditioning or a purification practice is essential. We need to erase everything we have gathered since childhood days!

Don't wait, bow to Maharaj now

Q. I have been wondering if spiritual experiences such as visions or other aspects were fundamental to the path? To date, I have not yet had any visions or experiences. Is this an indicator that I need to intensify the *sadhana*? This does not discourage me from continuing the practice, but let's say, it intrigues me. Maybe too little time has passed and I shouldn't rush. I know they are just concepts, to be honest, but I admit that I have a desire to have a vision of Maharaj and be able to bow at his feet. Patience, the will of the supreme be done.

A. It is different for everyone. It has nothing to do with not doing enough practice or having to wait longer. Some may have many experiences and others a few or maybe none. There is no need to wait for a vision of Maharaj. Bow to him now. Maharaj is with you. His presence is everywhere all around you, within you. What are you waiting for?

Q. I go from moments of extreme tranquillity where I desire nothing, to moments where the mind offers me visions of all kinds, even very ugly ones. I don't give it much weight, but how is it possible? On Saturday they broke the glass of my car, perhaps to steal and I didn't give it any thought. No reaction! I took the car to be repaired. No feelings of panic or anxiety for the very high cost! The next day, when I hadn't had any sexual desires for months and couldn't look at any woman, suddenly there was an onslaught of sexual thoughts. All kinds came to me! This monkey mind always seems to be at war with itself. Tell me is this normal, is this part of the process? Or am I doing something wrong in my *sadhana*?

A. Yes! It is normal. In time, with continuing practice, there will be no fluctuations or reactions at all. At the moment, you are undergoing a cleansing process. Instability will continue, until every last morsel of the ego mind has dissolved. You are not doing anything wrong. Have patience and determination!

Q. I heard you on one of the Satsangs criticizing someone. It is not good to criticise anyone. You are a True Master. Nisargadatta says that a true Master never criticises anyone.

A. It is not criticism. It is the duty of the Master to point out the ego at work and make someone aware!

Q. I have decided not to contact you for the next six months. This will give me a chance to dive deep into the practice, without reporting to you.

A. If that is what you are going to do, then all well and good. But you may start drifting and not even be aware that you are. It sounds like the mind is tricking you into disconnecting from me, so as it can get up to more mischief!

Don't divide yourself

Q. I feel centred during meditation. It is going very well. But my living circumstances and family life are full of chaos. And when I am involved with others, I cannot stay centred or keep in touch with Selfless Self.

A. Don't divide yourself into two between the meditator and the family man. To say your circumstances are full of chaos means that you are taking it all for real and allowing yourself to be dragged back into the illusion. The fact that you lose touch with your centre, with Reality, when you are around others means you have not absorbed the knowledge sufficiently. When the knowledge is absorbed, the switch between the meditator and family man will be seamless and you will remain centred at all times and untouched.

Q. I have lost interest in everything and it is a good feeling. Throwing out the non-essentials through the practice has brought me to this space.

A. You have been stripping away everything that is not part of your true nature. That is very good to hear.

Q. I have been doing intense practice and now when I close my eyes there is nothing, absolutely nothing there. It is like I vaporize. Is that normal? The last couple of days, I have not been able to use the Mantra because of this profound sense of nothingness. But it is a little destabilizing.

A. The process is different for everyone. Remember that all experiences are illusory. Don't worry about it! This experience, like all the others, will pass!

Q. During my practice, I felt reality slipping away. It was very uncomfortable, as if I was losing myself.

A. It was not reality that was slipping away, but illusion. And you felt uncomfortable because what was slipping away was all that you are familiar with, everything you know. You were entering unknown territory. There is nothing to fear! Be brave and take a leap!

Q. I am in the middle of the clearing process and now I'm feeling a little depressed. It is as if I'm losing all interest in things that used to be of interest.

A. This lack of interest or indifference is just a stage in the process and will pass. First of all, we need to detach ourselves from all the illusory things that we hold dear. But later on, after a shift in perspective, that sense of indifference will dissolve, too.

Q. I have been following the practice for several months now. How can I tell if I'm making progress or not?

A. You may find that you are more patient and tolerant of others. You may feel more enthusiastic about the meditation practice. And say, when you are faced with worldly difficulties and challenges, you will be less reactive and affected, than you were in the past.

Forget past practices

Q. As I recite the Mantra, I am trying to focus on the space between the thoughts?

A. Why are you doing that? I did not tell you to do that. This kind of meditation is different to what you have been used to. This process is about emptying yourself of all the illusory layers and concepts. In this very early stage, it is not about becoming more peaceful or blissful. We are using the Mantra as a hammering tool to dissolve the ego. So, please clean the slate and forget about past practices. Just follow my instructions.

Q. When thoughts arise, I push them down. Is that ok?

A. No! Don't force anything. When thoughts arise, just don't give them your attention. Use the Mantra and mantra your way through them!

Q. Life is so busy at the moment with work and family. And I am going on holiday for a few weeks. These long journeys are always stressful.

A. Remind yourself that you are not going anywhere. It is only the body that moves from A to B, not you. Nothing is, in fact, happening. You have lost touch with Selfless Self. When you think you are the doer, every hurdle seems like a big mountain to climb. Keep reminding yourself that you are not the doer.

Who feels remorse?

Q. When a seeker again gets involved in duality by following the illusory ego-mind and commits, for example, some ungodly actions, or shows emotions of anger, aggression, intemperance, etc. And then after reflecting and realising that he has been caught on the hook again, there comes a moment of repentance for what he has done... What is better? Remorse and repentance to Selfless Self, for having again identified with the ego mind and engaging in duality...or to stick to the position and convince oneself that nothing is happening, nothing has happened...that I am not a doer and there are no deeds...that I am not guilty of anything?

A. There has to be somebody to feel remorse and repentance. You are nobody. Definitely not remorse and repentance. Stick to the position and resolve to stay more alert, so that you do not fall into duality as often!

Q. I feel that I am playing a waiting game. I'm waiting for life to get better and for my circumstances to improve. This makes meditation nearly impossible!

A. Don't focus on the one who is waiting. Stay with the witness or knower of that. The one who is waiting is the pseudo self. Try and distance yourself from that illusion and you will be able to meditate again.

Don't be so hard on yourself

Q. I lament the fact that everything has changed. It was going so well with my meditation practice and deepening conviction. It felt as if my conviction had really grown and was strong. These days it is very difficult to meditate. Sometimes I miss it completely. Now I feel I've lost all that! It's like it has all gone!

A. Don't let the mind entrap you! You have made great inroads with your practice. Your conviction was strong because many layers of illusion had been erased. And during this process, a strong foundation of Reality was established within you. This foundation is solid and still remains. It cannot disappear! Nothing has changed and you have not lost anything. How can it all be gone? It is only that which is illusory and impermanent that disappears. Don't be too hard on yourself when you miss a practice. Try shorter sessions. All that is going on are a few clouds that have temporarily obscured your vision. Be assured that when the clouds disperse, you will be able to pick up where you left off, and even more than that!

Q. While I was sitting meditating, my body started to ache and my mind was screaming and telling me to stop. But I did not listen and carried on meditating. Eventually, the pain subsided. And as I forgot about the mind and the body, a blissful state followed.

A. Excellent! Your perseverance brought rewards. Here in this little battle with the mind, you became the victor and showed the mind that you are the Master, and not its slave. Well done!

Listen with an open heart

Q. I have read so many spiritual books from different traditions and now I feel as if they have just filled my head with unnecessary knowledge. This cleansing process would be easier if I had not accumulated so much! In your presence, it is all so simple. You share truth and I accept it... from Presence to Presence, heart to heart.

A. That is best. Don't think about what I am saying. Instead, listen with an open heart and drink it all in. In this way, the seed of truth is planted and will grow, spontaneously, without any interference from the mind.

Q. I have kept up the practice for a couple of years amidst a busy life. And I'm thinking that the Spontaneous Conviction should have happened by now. I'm beginning to lose heart.

A. Who is thinking that? Don't think! It will happen. Continue with the practice and know, that with grace, everything will unfold as it is meant to.

Only half the picture

Q. I know, and I have the conviction that everything is an illusion but this space is not very pleasant. It is not what I was expecting. It feels very dry and cold!

A. Knowing that everything is an illusion is only part one or half the picture. The other half is the Spontaneous Conviction that you are *Brahman*, the one and only

Reality, the Ultimate Truth, and, being established in that. The Spontaneous Conviction has not yet arisen! But when it does, there will be an overpowering sense of awe, overwhelming happiness, peace and love. Don't stop now! Keep moving forward, without analyzing what is happening or not happening.

Your "get out of jail card"

Q. I have begun to let my practice fall away. Today your divine call was appreciated.

A. Don't let it fall away. The longer you leave the practice, the harder it is to get back on it! What is the purpose of your meditation practice? Do you wish to stay imprisoned in the illusory world with all its ups and downs, or do you wish to discover the everlasting peace that you are? When you are tempted to let go of the practice, remind yourself that it is your doorway to freedom, the only "get out of jail card".

Q. When I am with you, and you explain the process, it feels very exciting and easy. But on my own…

A. Enough! You are doing it again… entertaining doubts! You are not on your own! Just remember my words, and if you do get stuck, don't hesitate to message me. I am here to lift you up when you stumble! Don't let pride stop you from reaching out!

Q. I don't want to trouble you as you have many devotees needing your attention.

A. It is no trouble! That's what I'm here for! Best to reach out before the ego grips you and controls you! Contact me before you become firmly and hopelessly entrapped by *Maya*! Because by then, you will no longer be able to initiate contact!

Have courage!

Q. You say that all I have to do is remove the layers of illusion and then my true nature will be revealed. It sounds very simple! But then you say that courage and determination are needed. Why?

A. The principle is easy to understand: You are already realized but your natural state has been covered by layers and layers of influences, conditioning, brainwashing. We have learned to respond and behave in certain ways. We have accepted so many concepts and lived an illusory life for many years. Therefore, when we undergo self-transformation, we are faced with many challenges including anxiety and the fear of letting go of all that we think we know, all that we imagine ourselves to be. The process can feel like a big conflict, as we attempt to let go of everything we know, everything that has given us a false sense of security. If we are not determined, we may just give up and convince ourselves that it is too difficult and befriend illusion again. Similarly, if we do not have courage, we may be overcome by illusory fear and abandon the practice altogether.

Let your children be free!

Q. I am bringing up my children, teaching them and influencing them in the way I would have liked to have been influenced. They see me sitting quietly and so, they imitate me and stay quiet. It is important I think at a young age to bring them up with spiritual values and a calm environment.

A. Children need to be given the freedom to explore the world and develop and grow, spontaneously. At that beautiful, never to be repeated, age of innocence, they should be allowed to express themselves and make noises, laugh aloud, scream and shout. Make sure there is a balance at home for funtime or playtime.

By imposing a rule of silence at home, if only indirectly, it is a type of suppression which is not healthy. At this tender, impressionable age, they will already be learning to repress the natural flow of expression because they have been taught that mum or dad will get angry, if they don't stay quiet. There are many years ahead for you to share the spiritual values you hold. For now, let them also have some fun! Let them be free!

Q. You seem to contradict yourself. You gave me one answer to a question and then I heard you give a different answer to the same question to someone else!

A. There are no contradictions. What I said to you was right and so was what I said to the other person. Both answers were correct and needed to be heard at the time!

Plus, I don't remember what I said to you. Whatever response is given flows out and is then forgotten.

Book knowledge is not your knowledge

Q. I seem to be drifting away from the practice, sometimes for a week or two, though I do find that your Q&A's are very helpful. Every day I read Nisargadatta and Ramakant. I know it is all about the books!

A. Try not to let it go for so long! I thought you were going to say, a day or so! And it is not all about the books! As long as the knowledge remains book knowledge, it means that the knowledge is not your own. Maybe the Q&A's help more because they are immediate.

A spiritual breakfast is essential

Q. Distractions, like family life, are stopping me from meditating. I used to get up very early and meditate but I have not been doing it for a while. But I hope to get back to it.

A. You can't let it go for so long. Don't take life for granted. If something happens to the body and you have not fully woken up, then another dream is bound to happen. As Maharaj repeated, again and again, casual spirituality will not work! At least, meditate in the morning, to give yourself a good chance to stay centred throughout the day. It is like having a good breakfast! Nourish the spirit first thing in the morning, and that way, you will not fall so easily into illusion throughout the day.

Q. The Q&A's are wonderful because I see there are others who have the same struggles as I do, and even just knowing that, has the effect of making me feel that I am not alone! It gives me both comfort and hope.

A. Good to hear! Now that it is nearly a year since they began, I am currently collating them for another book.

Q. I watched *Selfless Self*, the documentary film about Maharaj and love it. It is a work of love, thank you. I have watched it twice.

A. Watch it, again and again. It is not just a documentary. When you see Maharaj, you are receiving *darshan*, a transmission from the Master. Watch it with your heart! See it like that! Watch it more often, immerse yourself in it, and let Maharaj fill your heart, from Presence to Presence!

Fear

Q. I have some anxiety and fear when I meditate. Not to begin with, but as I go deeper into the meditation, I feel strong feelings of fear, even panic, that I am going to disappear, lose myself.

A. You know that the meditation practice is designed to dissolve the illusion of all that you think you are. Even though the fear is not real, it is normal to experience it, until there is the Conviction that you are not this body-mind, that you were never born and you will never die.

Q. If all the layers of illusion are erased, I mean, if I am erased then I am afraid that I won't be able to function in the world. Is that not the case?

A. Here you are believing yourself to be the doer which is an illusion. You were never the doer. Everything happens spontaneously. You do not make things happen. Without the power of Presence, you cannot function.

Knee-jerk reactions disappearing

Q. I have noticed some changes. Those things that I used to desire are much less now, eg., before if I wanted to buy a new iphone, I would buy it. There was no way I would not. Now that knee jerk reaction has gone. The desires are much less.

A. Yes what happens is a loosening of attachments and attractions to worldly things. And slowly, slowly, you become more inward and able to remain as the witness. As the witness you can observe yourself, look at the world from a distance, one removed and watch the movie, instead of your being part of it, deeply entrenched in it, as you were before. There is detachment, observing, whereas before the seen and the Seer were virtually entangled. Now the Seer is more detached from the seen. You are more relaxed which means that you do not get drawn so easily into illusion. You are making good progress. Continue with the hammering and absorbing the teachings, contemplating them and convincing yourself that you are not the body-mind, that you are not your name or persona, that you never were.

You are love itself

Q. How can I stay in love and be love at all times?

A. Your very nature is love, peace and happiness. When the "I" has dissolved, then you will not need to make any efforts to stay in love because you are not separate from love. You are love itself.

Q. How long do I need to meditate and sing *bhajans* for?

A. Until there is Conviction. The purification process you are undergoing is essential to hammer the ego and remove all the illusory layers, until you come to the realization that you are That! And then you will look back and laugh at how seriously you took yourself and everything else, including all the changing moods of sadness, depression, etc.

Show some maturity!

Q. You told me some time ago that soon, after some meditation, I would start to see changes taking place. Well, I still don't feel anything, except that I am wasting my time.

A. Coming to me complaining that you are wasting your time is the wrong attitude, the wrong approach. No one is forcing you to meditate. You came to me! Show some maturity. It was only some weeks ago that we spoke. You cannot expect to undo a lifetime's programming in a few weeks. Be patient!

Signposts

Q. How will I know if the process is coming to an end, if I am getting closer to the destination?

A. There will be signs such as growing tolerance and patience. Those things or people who used to annoy and irritate you, will no longer bother you. There will be a growing eagerness to know Reality, and with that, an increasing power of discernment. This means that you will not fall into the trap of illusion as much as before because your foundations will be solid. Also, there will be a loss of interest in certain worldly things that you used to enjoy and derive pleasure from. This happens as you are absorbing the knowledge and enjoying an increase in internal peace. As the destination nears, devotion increases, propelled by the longing to know oneself. And finally, there is Spontaneous Conviction.

Conviction

Q. What is Conviction?

A. When we listen to the knowledge of our Ultimate Truth, read and absorb it, along with allowing the Mantra vibration to convince us, while at the same time, convincing ourselves, this is the way of Conviction.

First, the seed of Conviction is an intellectual one, then gradually, with practice, as we accept it deeply - not with the mind, but with the core of our being, the Spontaneous Conviction arises. But it will not arise until all the body-based knowledge we have accumulated, has been completely erased, dissolved.

Auto-suggestion

Q. Can spontaneous belief come from continuous suggestion? After all, millions of people believe in non-existent things imparted by their family?

A. The answer is yes. Throughout our lives, we have been influenced by suggestion after suggestion. We have been programmed by many concepts. We were told that we are of the female sex or male sex, body minds, this age or that, this religion or that. In other words, we have been brainwashed. What we're doing at the moment is reversing the process by hammering ourselves with the truth of "I am *Brahman, Brahman* I am" instead of I am this or that.

We are undergoing a process of brainwashing ourselves, undoing the conditioning that we underwent as children and adults and replacing or supplanting the illusion, with the reality of "I am *Brahman*". That is what we're doing. It is as you say, auto-suggestion. Maharaj says that first you have to convince yourself and use the intellect to do that, and then in time, the Conviction will arise, spontaneously. But the hammering is really basic and necessary. We just have to keep hammering, hammering, hammering.

Q. As I deepen spiritually, will my external situation improve?

A. When the Conviction of your Truth, your Reality, deepens, when the inner work is taking place and moving forward, then you will also see the external affairs or material issues, changing in your favour. Basically, you will be looked after always and in all ways.

See the spiritual path as passionate and joyful!

Q. When there is Conviction all will be fine, but in between, well, it is frightening. There is nothing in life to captivate you. In the spiritual realm, you are only a work in progress. I guess we still have our responsibilities to take care of and that is the sole thing that can make us get up from our bed and go to the office and live life. In that, if we have issues in the family life as well, the motivation is that much less. So, based on other circumstances, the spiritual path can be a dreary path. Probably when I see you, my spirits will be boosted.

A. How can you say that? It is not a dreary path at all. It is passionate and joyful! The drive to know oneself, to wake up from the dream is a lively, powerful one. There should be a feeling of longing and gratification, that you are getting closer and closer to Truth. To be as you are, to, "just be" is not empty and nihilistic. It is emptiness filled with happiness. You are letting the mind dictate to you again and listening to negative thoughts. They are not true, so, stop paying attention to them!

Q. When Maharaj uses the word "Conviction", does he mean realization – directly experiencing the truth that "*I am Brahman*"?

A. When Maharaj uses the word "Conviction", he means knowing that you are That. It is a direct knowing of your Reality, a firm Conviction. First of all, the Conviction is worked at, ie., intellectually. We are convinced by the Knowledge we are absorbing and simultaneously, we are convincing ourselves, with the aid of the practice tools. But the Final Conviction arises spontaneously. And once this occurs, it is permanent, established as an unequivocal certainty of knowing with the totality of one's being, that you are *Brahman*.

Q. How will I know when I have the Conviction. To be honest, I don't feel it is there yet. I am still just trying to convince myself.

A. When it happens you will know because you will no longer have to convince yourself. The Conviction will arise spontaneously and remain. What you are doing is right. The process of conviction begins intellectually. We need to constantly tell ourselves, remind ourselves of our Reality. Then the time will come, with the help of reciting the Mantra, when the Conviction arises, naturally and spontaneously.

Bootcamp

Q. Can you speak about the importance of Bootcamp and what Maharaj referred to as the "Spiritual Cocktail"?

A. Bootcamp means practical training. It is an essential, cleansing process that will undo and remove all the illusory layers and add-ons that have attached themselves to your Presence. This is done by using a combination of practices - or what Maharaj called a spiritual cocktail of "Self-enquiry, Mantra recitation, Meditation and Devotion. Without bootcamp, there cannot be a purification process which means that spiritual knowledge will just sit on top of the ego, instead of being absorbed. These practices will remove the thoughts, ideas, points of view, stances, impressions – everything that was acquired by the body-mind. It is essential that the ground is completely cleared and cleaned before planting any seeds. Nothing will grow in the soil unless you root out all the weeds produced from ignorance that were taking up your precious space. Sweep away all these fake seeds because they are not part of your essential nature. They are not part of who you are, and will prevent the flower of Truth from blossoming. We need to use some tools such as "Self-enquiry", "Reciting a Mantra", "Meditating", as well as "Devotion and singing Kirtan/*Bhajans*".

Put briefly, the practice of Self-enquiry, using *neti neti* is essential for you to find out first-hand, what you are not. Then you can remove everything about yourself that is not true. The Mantra's job is one of hammering the ego. A mantra is a concentration tool that weakens the resistant mind. Reciting a mantra lets the mind know who is in charge and running the whole show, i.e., the authentic ruler!

Meditation is necessary to establish your Reality. Here, basic meditation involves churning the knowledge of your Reality – that you are unborn, limitless, the Source, prior to beingness, etc. - and not letting your concentration stray. It means keeping your attention fixed on your Reality, until that Ultimate Reality that you are is permanently established. And when this happens, you will no longer need to put in any effort.

Listening to, or singing kirtan/*bhajans*, will also help you absorb the knowledge. It is another effective medium that will keep the thoughts at bay, while at the same time creating and maintaining a happy and uplifting atmosphere.

Together, these tools work to remove all the illusory layers, similar to the way a potent cocktail removes our inhibitions! The overall aim is to supplant the idea, the false notion of "I am the body", with the Truth of "I am Ultimate Reality". If this Truth just remains theoretical, it will not work. There has to be a deep and direct Conviction. In other words, there must be total acceptance. All these aids are necessary to kick the old tenants out of your house, bring about a successful shift in perspective, and eventually, take you out of duality.

Let the mind follow you!

When you were trapped in the imaginary world, you identified with people, places and things which kept you in a constant state of flux. You became slaves of the mind, the ego, and the intellect. With practice, you will stop listening to the old records, and go against the flow. You will no longer have to follow the mind but instead, turn it around and develop the habit of letting the mind follow you! Bootcamp's primary aim is to disempower the mind and reveal your Original, Stateless State: You are unborn. You are prior to beingness!

Asking the question, "Who am I?" is the most critical question you can ask because it opens the door to the Infinite. When you sift through all of your concepts, shake them up and loosen your attachments to the false and the transient, then your natural, endless Source will open up and reveal itself. Self-enquiry helps to shift your attention from the imaginary world of the seen, to the Seer. It removes the obstacles that are taking up space and cluttering up your vastness: the incessant noise of the mind that prevents you from hearing the silence. When that disturbing hum stops and the thoughts lessen, a pure and beautiful silent space will emerge.

Self-enquiry is particularly useful in the beginning of the process of dismantling all the ideas and notions you have about yourself. While you cannot stop the thoughts from flowing, as that is the nature of the mind, nevertheless, you can catch them before they catch you, before they have had a chance to leave their impressions, or begin to multiply.

What are the aims of the Self-Enquiry process? Discrimination and discernment between the false and the real. Self-Enquiry frees us from our illusory, mental prisons, disempowers and reduces our thoughts and brings about the disappearance of the illusory thinker. That primary "I-thought" (mind/ego) is the culprit responsible for identifying with all the thoughts and concepts. It is the hook on which all the other thoughts and ideas hang. That pseudo-ego has only managed to survive because we have been giving all our attention and interest to the thoughts, without any discrimination. All thought is unreal, and all thought is fleeting. You are prior to consciousness, prior to thought, prior to words.

Melting the illusory you

Mantra - You can view a mantra as the thorn that will remove the existing, unwanted thorn. The current thorn is "I am the body" (and its replacement is "I am Ultimate Reality"). The continuous reciting of a mantra hammers the ego and effectively dissolves body-based knowledge, eventually establishing you as Ultimate Reality. This kind of hammering or repetition of your Reality establishes you in your Truth. Eventually, you will realize that nothing exists except Selfless Self. There is nothing apart from Selfless Self. There is only one Principle. You are That!

Reciting a Mantra such as "*Aham Brahmasmi*" or "*I am Brahman, Brahman I am*", will dissolve your strong thoughts and concepts, melting the remnants of the illusory you, who still considers yourself to be somebody! Reciting a Mantra can be seen as a corrective process that acts as a constant reminder of who/what you are. It will help take you out of illusion and eventually pave the way back Home. Let it do its thing and uproot all your buried hurts and memories of, e.g., anger, violation, betrayal, injustice etc. Put an end to your suffering by disidentifying from the body-form, and going beyond your illusory wounds and scars.

Reciting a mantra is a simple antidote to illusion. How do these mantras work? By engaging the mind and stopping activity. Intellectual and egoistic activity stop spontaneously with the reciting of the mantra. At the same time, Spirit-Presence begins to flow outwards, as it is reminded of its identity, its Reality. When you adopt this practice, the mind quietens down, and a peaceful space comes to the fore. Don't strain your brain trying to understand how it works, or if it is working at all, just continue to recite the mantra, with total commitment and concentration.

Calmly reflect on your true identity

Meditation - Meditation on your true nature will deepen your understanding, enabling you to dwell as your natural state, in that field of Reality. How do you do that? For example, contemplate the truth of "I am Ultimate Reality!" What does it mean? What are the implications? Ponder this! There is only one Reality and you are that Reality. If everything is that Reality, that means everything is within you. Ponder this! Let that truth touch your heart! Or practice churning the powerful truth: "I am prior to beingness", or "I am unborn".

Calmly reflect on your true identity, that Stateless State before beingness, in this way: "I exist! I have always existed, but not as a body-mind. How was I?" Meditating like this draws you closer to your unidentified identity. Here, you are not looking for answers, but instead, tapping into your transcendent nature, your Source, and bathing in that sacred atmosphere, that river of Light.

At the advanced stage, when there is nothing left to dwell upon - because the gap between knowing and being has been bridged, you will be established in your natural state (without the you of course). And when this happens, your efforts will no longer be needed.

When knowing and being are one

Meditation in the real sense is not something you can do; it is indwelling, synonymous with what you are. When knowing and being are one, only then, is real abidance possible, day and night, night and day, in that unlimited Self that you are.

Practice meditation: remembering and dwelling on your true identity 24/7 and keeping the focus of your attention on the Source. Concentrate on your Essence, your Reality. Stay with your Reality at all times. With practice, meditation will become a way of spontaneously living life as you are in your true Essence, at one with the Source that is your Reality. Don't involve yourself in any thought processes. Why would you, when you have nothing to do with that! You are nothing to do with that. You are the witness that is always standing at the bank of the river. You are not flowing with the thoughts, but letting them pass by like a meandering river. Don't take delivery of them. Don't be upset by them. Don't judge them!

The illusory triad

Devotion - Devotion includes *puja* or worship to the Masters, bowing to them, surrendering to them, expressing your gratitude as well as devotional singing. When you are singing, the mind quietens down. Singing *bhajans* connects us to our divinity, to the one Source. They are not expressions of worshipping an external Deity because there is only one Reality. You are That!

You are that Presence, that Selfless Self, that Inner Guru you are singing to, singing about, and for want of a better word, that you are "worshipping". Here, the illusory triad of worship, worshipper and worshipped, are, of course, one and the same. You are all three in one! With Conviction, you are giving praise to yourself. You are filled with gratitude, love and pure joy because you know everything is within you. And not only that, you wish to express your thanks and humility. In other words, you are blessing yourself in recognition of the supreme opportunity you have been given to know yourself! *Bhajans* or Kirtans celebrate your Selfless Self. They plug you into your Source.

If you take bootcamp seriously, you will witness a beautiful self-transformation. And when the pseudo self is demolished, your training at Bootcamp will be finished! For a fuller explanation please see the "Practice" section in the first *Who Am I?* book.

How long is a piece of string?

Q. How long does it take to realize the Ultimate Truth?

A. How long is a piece of string? It takes various lengths of time because it all depends on how involved we are in the practice, how seriously we take it, how mature we are spiritually, and how hungry we are to know ourselves. If we are very casual about our search and practice, then it could take a very long time. However, if we're passionate and driven, earnest and determined, it could happen quickly.

The best thing to do is to live each day, as if it were your last, accompanied by a gentle pressure to wake up from the dream. If you approach the process too casually, and tell yourself that next day or next week or next month, you will get to grips with who you are, then there may not be a next week or next month. So, I would advise you to approach your search with an attitude of urgency. Urgency coupled with a longing for truth is the perfect combination.

Who is interested in the world?

Q. I'm still interested in what goes on in the world. I have preferences, I'm interested in world affairs. Participating in the world in this way, is this taking the touch of this waking dream, or does it come under the header of doing my duty?

A. If you're taking an interest in the world, then you're taking everything for real. You are taking yourself for real. You're taking the world for real. You're enjoying the scenery – that which you see, instead of staying with the Seer. The practice involves staying with the Seer at all times and not being dragged into the world. Now it sounds by this question that you're enjoying the entertainment. The mind is enjoying the entertainment, but if you continue taking the world for real, you are allowing the days, weeks and months to slip by. You're taking each day for granted and it's not helping you.

You need to attend, go within, look within. Stop looking at the world! It's the only way to find out who you are. Do your practice! So there needs to be more Self-enquiry about who is still interested in the world? Who is it who has preferences? Really get to grips with the practice! None of us know how long we have left in the body, so we can't go around swanning in the world. Our priority is that we are here on this Earth to wake up! That's the only reason we're here! And if we don't wake up from the dream, there will be another dream followed by another dream. So, why not use the body as the vehicle for Self-Realization instead of for worldly pleasures, enjoyment and stimulation for the mind. Just do the practice. Maharaj has given us all the tools. He has shown us the way. We have all the instructions. We just have to follow them. If you're sincere and dedicated, Self-realization will happen. Don't waste time! All we have is now!

Q. Does the individual have free will?

A. Well, there is no individual, therefore, who has free will? The individual is an illusion. Free will is a concept. Everything happens spontaneously. There are no separate beings, no separate individuals. There is only one Essence and we're all part of the same essence. We are all formless.

Nisargadatta Maharaj definition of "Consciousness"

Q. Is ego part of the Consciousness?

A. Remember that you are prior to language. "Ego", "Consciousness", all these words create confusion! The answer depends on how you define "Consciousness". If it is defined as the Reality, then the answer would be "No". But if we use Nisargadatta and Ramakant Maharaj's definition that we are prior to Consciousness, then the answer is "Yes". The ego is part of Consciousness. Nisargadatta distinguishes between Consciousness and Awareness. Consciousness cannot exist without Awareness but Awareness exists without Consciousness. Here Awareness means the Absolute Reality that is completely separate from the illusory "I".

The ego is the pseudo "I". It is what we have constructed as ourselves, what we have made of ourselves through influences and impressions from the world. The ego is the false "I", a product of conditioning which has blinded us and made us into who we think we are. Our practice involves the destruction of the ego, by removing all the layers, so that we can uncover our true reality.

Q. If Oneness is all there is and there is a body mind and even an ego, then it must have come from Oneness. That's how I felt… that's what I thought, that the ego could still be… if there's only one then it only can be part of the one.

A. Consciousness can be understood as a reflection through the body. The ego comes with the manifestation of the body form which is the separation from Oneness into the body form, falling into the illusion of being separate individuals. Therefore, we all develop separate egos. The job we have is to dissolve the ego because it's just a covering or sheath on our true self. When we manifested as the body form, we separated from Source and then we believed ourselves to be the body form, the ego, the ego mind, whatever you wish to call it. It's a covering, layers of covering, layers of conditioning that we need to uncover, remove, before returning to the Source.

Don't get too friendly with the ego

Q. That's partly answered it for me. I mean I know it's ego talking now so that's off the issue, but for me, when I saw the Oneness of it all and you have that formless nothingness that's everything, then for me, it was

Oneness objectified. I know it's a vision or visionary, or what we call it, a phenomenon so to speak, but still, it's just for me, it was a changing state, let's say, a temporary changing state from where we are absorbed back into a formless state.

But there is some kind of subject who is the "I am" for me and it's looking out and it's there as livingness through the individual forms that are within this actual universe. But I appreciate I'm talking from ego, yeah totally. I'm just trying to explain how I feel.

A. Definitely the ego is the problem and we need to resolve it. Where was the ego prior to beingness? We can always use that statement as a barometer to take us back to our natural State where there was nothing prior to being: no mind, no ego, no intellect, no nothing, no words, no language, no nothing. So, don't get too friendly with the ego!

Automatic responses

Q. My question is, if I realize, then there would be a fear that I would be almost a zombie within this universe. And for me, let's say, I say "Hello Annji". Then Annji has to respond to a name. And in order to respond to that name, for me there must be something left of an ego form that doesn't feel it's the doer. It's a non doer but it's a functional part. Therefore, that's what enables you to respond to what are illusionary objects and forms. Does that make any sense?

A. First of all, regarding realization, there's no one who realizes. Realization means liberation from the person. When the ego dies, realization happens. As long as you are there, as long as the personality is still there, then realization is not possible. And when you talk about names, the only reason we respond to our name is because we have been conditioned to do so. As babies, we were given a name and so the child responds, like one of Pavlov's dogs. It is like an automatic response. Somebody calls your name and you say "yes", and it's just conditioning, automatic. It has nothing to do with anything else. Because we respond to a name doesn't mean to say we believe that we are that name. We are nameless and formless.

Q. I recently watched a video with a collection of Shri Nisargadatta quotes where he referred to himself. He would often say: "Don't confuse me with who is talking right now. Don't confuse me with the body. You see a body but I don't. I hear questions and answers are coming. I'm hearing it just like you're hearing it". So, that's right, we can't even guess what that's like while we're in this ego trap. Yes, that was something that kind of hammered home for me that it's utterly beyond anything that we can say, as to what will I be like when I'm realized. It's not like that because there's no one there anymore! Just abide, abide as what one is always. I mean the words can't even talk about it anymore at that point.

A. To go back to fear. After Self-realization, how can you function in the world? Well, it doesn't happen like that because the process of Self-Realization is one of a shift in perception. Previously, you viewed the world in one way, afterwards, you view it in another way, but you don't become a sort of zombie. Without the "you" or "I", there is still functioning. It was always the Spontaneous Presence that was doing everything - not you, the doer, as you once thought. Because you used to think you were the doer of everything, now you are anxious that you will lose yourself. But when the ego mind/persona has dissolved, functioning will continue.

Develop the conviction that you are not the doer and understand that without the Spontaneous Presence, the body is just a dead body. Grow in conviction that it's the Presence, the one Presence behind everything that allows you to function in the world. The Presence is the power. You are that power. There is no power in the ego mind. When Conviction is established, then all these thoughts and fears of yours will dissolve because you will no longer be attached, no longer identified with your false identity.

Q. Intellectually, I have no problem with losing my pseudo identity. Honestly, he is not that fantastic! And I do not have a problem with saying intellectually, that I am not the doer, so that is progress in a way. I'm trying to know what is unknowable almost up to that point, yeah, and that's where my questions were coming from. But yes, more and more every day, I feel as though there's a lessening of me and more of it will take place.

Oneness is happening. I'm not doing anything. In fact, I don't even exist. As daft as that might sound to other people. Beyond this group, this or that mindset, I do not believe that I exist. It's almost like a game... maybe the practice is working and helping the user to dissolve the attachments one by one, little by little. It's the process we all go through. It works and the conviction will come.

Q. How and why are we the way we are? Some people are like skilled at some things. They have different strengths and weaknesses, maybe different tendencies. Good at some things. bad at others.

A. This question is really to do with body-based knowledge and not what we're discussing here. Because when we know that we're not the body-mind, and we remove all the layers, then all this learned behaviour or self-perception of ourselves ie., good at this, bad at that... all of it will disappear. Duality will dissolve, so it's not really a big issue. That's all I have to say about that.

Only four hours per day to realize my divinity

Q. 200-300 years back, our occupation was an extension of our self. Now we have earmarked some hours of our day, to go to the office to earn a living. And this time is untouchable as it is dedicated to our employers. Full time dedication to the divine or Self-enquiry seems impossible during these work hours. In the present state of humanity, if 10 hours are dedicated to work and 8 hours to sleep, 2 hours, say for travelling, then only 4 hours are available to realise the divinity within!

A. You are seeing yourself as the doer and separating your time at work from your reality. You have not established yourself as the witness and are taking it all for real. Instead, realize that you are simply playing different roles – as an employee, travelling to work, etc.

Death

Q. I imagine that at the time of death, most people have some fear because they are facing the unknown and therefore, they feel very alone?

A. No! Not at all! If you have died to the ego before the end of your bodily existence, then there is no one there to be fearful. Who is going to be afraid? On the contrary, the last moment can be the opposite – blissful, the fulfilment of a lifetime because finally, there is complete separation from the body-form! And not only that, because of our link to the Masters in this Lineage, they will ensure that we are not alone. They will be with us in the final moments.

I experienced this first hand from witnessing my late husband, Charles', final moments which I would like to share with you. In 2018, some days before leaving the body, Nisargadatta Maharaj would appear to him and make his presence felt. He would remind Charles to "Welcome the difficulties", to which Charles replied with humour, saying, "Have I not had enough of them?"

And then at the point of his transition, I saw all the Lineage Masters gathered round his bed and they were clapping. And that is not all! On the day of his cremation, another miracle took place. As I was singing the *bhajans*, suddenly, Nisargadatta Maharaj appeared! He was blessing Charles, sprinkling him with deep rose red coloured petals. And then I saw the two of them merge and spiral round and round, before the vision disappeared! Both awestruck and excited, I bowed and burst out laughing at the same time! I was so grateful to Nisargadatta, that I knelt down and thanked him for the huge and timely blessing. There were no tears because I knew Charles had not gone anywhere. Where would he go? He just returned to the formless state!

In conclusion, we will have nothing to fear when it is our time, as long as we have erased the ego and woken up from this dream! And be assured that the Masters will be there to accompany us and receive us. Jai Guru!

The purpose of Self-enquiry is disidentification

Q. Often such thoughts come that I have some kind of roll back, as if a year ago or earlier, I was more spiritual. I tell myself to ignore these thoughts. That I was more spiritual is not true because the "I" is an illusion and as Maharaj teaches, the true meaning of spirituality is to hammer and demolish this "I" which is the false "I". Once the false "I" has been erased, then there is the emergence of what is truly spiritual. Another question, when I conduct Self-enquiry and ask a question, for example, "Who wants it? To whom did it come, etc.

Should I find and give an answer through reflection, seeing this is what someone wants, or this has come to that while taking the form of the ego? Or is self-exploration a system of sequential questions that at first have no answer and they have a cumulative effect after which one answer comes?

A. The purpose of Self-enquiry is not to find answers, as any answer you come up with will be illusory. Its purpose is to disidentify from the thoughts, concepts and attachments. For example, if we say, "To whom does this thought come?", by asking the question we are stopping the thought in its tracks. Before practicing Self-enquiry, we take our thoughts as being real, as if we are the thoughts, as well as the thinker behind them. But when we ask the question "to whom?", we are disconnecting ourselves from the thoughts. And when we do this more and more, we simultaneously believe in them less and less, and subsequently, give less attention to the thoughts. At the same time, they lose their power. That is the idea behind the Self-enquiry as a practice.

Q. I have already had thoughts or an understanding that I will not be able to realize myself as me. I will have to say goodbye to my identity and everything connected with me. I am theoretically ready for this and accept it, but still nothing happens. It seems to be a game of two roles. On the one hand, the seeker who in one period of wakefulness rejects everything and performs the practice, putting everything on the line, calling everything that happens, and is perceived as illusion. And on the other period of time, he is completely immersed in this illusion. In order to simplify things, he simply continues to exist and fulfil his duties. It seems work and family life offer great challenges for progress, for one not to be caught up in their demands.

A. The duties and work in daily life give you further practice to dissolve the "I" who still thinks it's the doer. Everything happens spontaneously. You need to remember this at all times. Applying the teachings to daily life is the practice. These teachings need to be lived, Only, when they are lived, can you gauge your progress. When there is absolute, solid conviction, you can be anywhere doing anything and always remain untouched. That pure, pristine energy, that reality that you are is immutable. It cannot be altered or blemished in any way. You need to know this and accept it. Your feelings of frustration or thoughts of abandoning work and family are part of the process. But know that these illusory feelings will also pass.

Don't compare!

Q. In the book *Timeless Years,* you write that the Presence of the Masters is very strong, sometimes even emitting a fizzing or sizzling sound. Could that sound also be described like the buzzing of bees? Was it non-local? Was it constant, although variable in volume?

A. You are trying to make a comparison with someone else's experiences. It is pointless. Even if it were the same as yours, you know that experiences are illusory. They come and go. Therefore, don't waste time on them.

Maharaj's humour

Q. Would you share some stories about Ramakant Maharaj and his sense of humour?

A. Okay! A few years after we met Maharaj, we told him that before our Tuesday afternoon Skype sessions, fear started rising and our stomachs were upset because we were afraid as 4 o'clock approached. There were feelings of dread. Maharaj's tone was so innocent, as if to say, how could you possibly be afraid of me? As if he couldn't hurt a fly. It was very funny!

Another one was when I returned in 2018 to the ashram and my birthday was approaching. The day before, Maharaj said, excitedly, in front of Anvita, "We have a surprise for you! Tomorrow we will celebrate your birthday in the ashram!" Again, he laughed like a child. Anvita was not pleased at all and she scolded him, saying, "Maharaj, now you have spoiled the surprise!" Maharaj just kept on smiling and laughing.

Because of his light, fun and humorous nature, we could joke with him. So, one day, when we were skyping with Maharaj and Charles was in a mischievous mood, he said to Maharaj, "Maharaj. we have a problem!" Immediately, Maharaj stopped smiling, became very serious and said: "Problem?" He didn't like the sound of that, obviously. And then, Charles said, "Yes Maharaj, we are too happy!" At that point, we all laughed together. It was a lovely moment of oneness and joy!

So, these are a few examples, a taste of his humour and his easy-going nature.

Radical measures

Q. I want to ask about the place for radical measures. In his books, Shri Ramakant Maharaj says that until all bodily knowledge, all concepts are eliminated, the truth, the reality will not be revealed. Nevertheless, some seekers believe and hope that some radical measures including, for example, the use of entheogen plants containing substances that change consciousness such as mushrooms cacti, aasa, etc, can accelerate, bring closer or even give Self-realization help to realize the truth. Therefore, can such or other radical measures be useful in establishing Reality?

A. Trying to hurry the process is not advisable. Consuming something from an external Source means that you are still caught up in illusion. Because whatever is taken will only have a temporary effect. These plants or drugs may open doors that one is not ready for. They may cause a blissful experience as well. Following the blissful ones, there is often a desire to re-experience them because they were so amazing! The question to ask is where were all these so-called consciousness-changing substances prior to beingness? There was nothing there.

The only way to find reality is by way of eliminating all the layers of illusion, turning within and knowing that everything is within you. You are the source of everything. If you start experimenting with substances, natural or not, then these will create further layers of impressions and delusion that need to be removed. Instead of accelerating the process, their influence is actually taking you backwards.

Are you willing to die for Truth?

Q. Why despite the fact that not a little effort is being made, the invisible listener who hears the truth about himself, the knowledge and other things that indicate his real Essence, he still does not accept his truth, his reality? Maybe he likes to experience these illusory experiences and therefore he is not in a hurry. It's like a genie who has been sitting in a lamp for thousands of years, switches on and can fully realize its potential in being.

A. It is a combination of both. Even though we wish to accept the knowledge and reality, the conditioning that we have undergone has left its mark. The person we grew up to be, the personality that was moulded took years. We cannot expect it to dissolve overnight. It will take some time. Secondly, we have grown attached to worldly things and experiences, and therefore, the familiarity, taste and enjoyment of them can still be appealing. Furthermore, while many may be interested in finding out the truth about who they are, there does not seem to be any urgency about it. They are not in a hurry. They are casual about it and continue to live life with one foot in the world and one foot in spirituality. That will not work, as Maharaj often said. There has to be seriousness and full involvement to wake up from the dream. And as Nisargadatta Maharaj said: "you need to be willing to die for truth".

New Concepts: "Aha" moments

Q. And what about new concepts that appear in the course of practice? For example, yesterday came the realization of how everything works, like the game of the five elements strikes different forms, and the Presence in contact with these forms bring them into action, into life. And thus, it exists forever, leaving one form. It is at this moment through another form and it is infinite. I just look at these ideas as other illusory thoughts and conclude what you describe as being more of a deepening of understanding.

A. Yesterday I was speaking with someone who said that during meditation what became clear to him was the actual reality of what nonduality means! That if there is not two, then he must be all. It was an "Aha" moment.
Yours is like an "Aha" moment, an understanding, a deeper insight. It is very good. It's not to be discarded along with the garbage. You should attach importance to this revelation because with the practice, comes more understanding which is what leads to Conviction. Know

better what to keep and what to throw out. It's important to use discrimination so that when you get lots of thoughts during the meditation, you recognise the ones that are actually teaching you. Don't just dump them all together with the rest of the rubbish. When they are teaching you things and giving you a deeper understanding, hold onto them.

True happiness is causeless

Q. I have everything going for me: a good job, a lovely wife and children. Yes, I am happy with all that most of the time, but I still feel that something is missing. Deep down, I am unhappy because I am not fulfilled.

A. The job, the wife and family are related to worldly happiness. You can't expect these things to bring you complete fulfilment. No one and nothing can give you that. True happiness is causeless. Complete fulfilment can only be found within you. You have accomplished yourself in your work and family life but are still feeling some kind of lack. You are now looking for something else. That something else you are looking for is that ultimate happiness that lies within you. Now you have reached the point where you need to find out who you really are! Because it is only through this search for truth that you will find complete fulfilment. When you know what you are, that you are not the body-mind, that you are unborn, eternal and the Source of happiness and peace, then you will be fulfilled and happy. And this kind of happiness is spontaneous and permanent!

Q. I don't feel I deserve to be happy because I am not a good person!

A. Who is saying this? First of all, your statement is not true. The "I" that is saying this is the false "I". and the person you talk about is simply a concept! You are not that. How can you say you do not deserve to be happy, when happiness is your nature! Peace is your nature! Whatever has already gone on in your life is illusory. Good and bad are concepts used in the world of duality. You are beyond all duality. Where was this "person" prior to beingness? Who says you don't deserve happiness? That is the ego talking and the ego is an illusion. You are not a person, individual or a separate entity at all. You are formless, eternal, beyond good and bad. Happiness is not something to acquire, it is your nature. Read *Who am I?* It is a very simple book that will help you understand how you developed these wrong notions about yourself and it will show you how to unravel all of them.

Existential Crisis

Q. I find this whole existence bemusing. During childhood and youth, we don't have doubts whether we are this body or not and we compete without harming anyone. Come older, middle age and the whole world seems against us and by that time, we are too impaired to fight. Add to that an existential crisis in terms of who we are and we have our cup of woe filled to the brim! But no intellectual answers are satisfactory. We have to have a spiritual catharsis to make sense of all this, I guess. Here's where the *Naam Mantra* comes in, I guess. May God give me the good sense to see it through. I know I have your blessing and the dust of your holy feet will see me through.

A. It need not be bemusing. When we are children, we do as we are told. We are influenced by parents, teachers, peers, in other words, we are programmed as body-minds and we take the world for real and everyone else. These are the layers that were superimposed on us. Then, as we mature, we attempt to find out what life is all about, it's meaning, and we search. And if we are spiritually inclined, we discover answers. We know intellectual answers will not suffice! There has to be a transformation which occurs through deprogramming all that was superimposed, and removing the layers till we uncover our innocence, true nature, as it was before we accepted all the illusion. And, of course, you have my blessings and my guidance which will see you through, no question! Have no doubt! There is nothing stopping you except your self-created doubts, therefore, don't entertain them! Jai Guru.

Q. I still feel depressed and sad sometimes, even though I have been practising for many months now.

A. Who is counting? A few months is nothing! Time is a concept. Deprogramming will take as long as is needed. Don't count the months! You have been programmed over a lifetime, you cannot expect total transformation overnight! We only feel depressed or sad, if we think we are somebody and take our feelings and the ups and downs of life for real. When, through the process of dissolving, you know that you do not exist as a person, and your true nature is revealed, then you will be liberated from your small self/ego. And when this happens, you will know that the Reality that you are is all that is... therefore, who is sad? Who is depressed? The result will be causeless, permanent happiness and no death...Who can die when you are unborn? Jai Guru!

Ramana, Nisargadatta, Ramakant – No duality!

Q. My problem is the long Ramana Maharshi influence. Somehow, I have to fully tread this path, without the hangover of the previous path. I have to believe that Bhagawan has led me to you and Maharaj. For me, this is the main challenge. I am at a crossroads of my spiritual *sadhana*. But I have to believe that Bhagawan Ramana sent me to you and Maharaj. Period! It is His wish that I follow the *Naam Mantra* and its assiduous practice with meditation. It is his wish that I take this giant leap of faith to transcend my human frailties. And I will do just that, even though my ego will play all sorts of tricks to wean me away. I have your help too. Thank you.

A. There is only one path. There is no conflict. Of course, Ramana led you to me and Maharaj. Remember Maurice Frydman and Jean Dunn? They were Ramana devotees and they both went to be with Nisargadatta who are one and the same. I keep telling you that the Guru is not the form. There is no duality. Stop thinking so much, stop torturing yourself. Just be at peace.

The ego loves an audience

Q. Sometimes, periodically, in conversations with relatives or acquaintances, when we exchange information, we talk about our daily lives, about family, etc. And the conversation gets to the point where what I'm talking about differs from, let's say, the generally accepted standards. For example, that I don't eat meat, or I don't plan to send my children to school. Naturally, this raises questions and I have to explain my point of view.

Then, as a rule, such conversations flow into the sphere of spirituality and I begin to talk about my spiritual beliefs. At the same time, I try not to quote the Masters, except in rare cases, when a specific example or quote is very appropriate and brings clarity as never before. I mainly use my spontaneous examples and principles of persuasion. But in one of his books, Nisargadatta Maharaj said that you do not need to share this Knowledge with anyone until you Realize, otherwise you will only make it worse for yourself. Why is it worse? What is the meaning of this "worse"? It seems to me that by convincing them or bringing information to them, I am also simultaneously convincing the Invisible Listener in me. Or is it worth avoiding such a thing?

A. You should avoid sharing this knowledge with others prior to Self-Realization. And even after Self-Realization, do not share it unless someone asks and is interested. Don't impose this knowledge on anyone! Why will sharing it prior to SR make it worse for you? Because when the Conviction is not yet there in you, this means that you have not absorbed the knowledge fully. Added to that, when you start sharing this knowledge with those who are unfamiliar with it, you have a perfect setting for the ego to rise up. The ego loves an audience. For you to be centre-stage and expound knowledge to the uninitiated, creates the possibility of inflating the ego and undoing some of the good work. Demonstrating what we know, even unintentionally showing off, is the opposite of humility.

Sharing this knowledge with family members and acquaintances can also make it worse for you because you are making yourself vulnerable in this circle. Their comments or criticisms can affect you and leave unwanted impressions. For example, the feedback you receive can raise doubts in you and destabilize you, even throw you off course.

Further, the process you are undergoing is your process, your business, not anyone else's. It is too early to share this knowledge when you have not absorbed it. I would carry out some Self-Enquiry and ask yourself why you wish to share this knowledge with the "wrong company"? Where is it coming from? Does the ego wish to show off? Does the ego wish to express his one-upmanship? Does the ego wish to challenge others? Where is this need to share coming from? Does the journey you are on make you feel lonely or isolated? In answer to your question, it is better to avoid such situations!

Operate as *Brahman*! Live as *Brahman*!

Q. I am patiently waiting for the Spontaneous Presence to reveal itself. Till such time, I feel life will keep running on the basis of the ego. It is treacherous, illusory, etc., but yet, I have to operate life through it. Can you suggest something by which I can make peace with the world and myself. Operating as the ego seems like torture and causes pain. But how can I make it bearable?

A. The whole point of the practice, i.e., Self-enquiry, reciting the Mantra and absorbing the knowledge is to stop you living life from an ego-driven body base! This knowledge of your reality clearly stated in *Selfless Self* which you are supposed to be absorbing, is to be applied to your daily life. You are not applying it! You seem to be waiting for something to happen, magically, without any effort on your part!

When you know the ego has been controlling you and it is false, you don't have to operate through it any longer! What is the point of awareness if you don't put it into practice? I feel that you go forward some days and then allow yourself to undo all the good work. Why are you operating as the ego, when you know better? Operate as *Brahman*! Live as *Brahman*! You are giving far too much attention to the changing, the illusory. And even though you know you are the Changeless Reality, you are not accepting it. You need to apply the teachings now! You need to stop listening to the old tapes going round and round in your head! Whenever your attention strays, bring it back to centre, to Selfless Self. If you don't follow the practice, then you are just keeping the door open for the ego to keep controlling you!

Peace comes from knowing that you are the eternal, immutable Source. It comes from knowing that nothing that happens in this changing world can touch your Reality, your Presence, that forever remains pristine, unblemished, pure! Don't let yourself be discouraged so easily!

If you don't have faith in the process, then it won't work! You give up very easily which does not help. And that is why I ask you if you are serious about Self-Realization? The fact is you are your own Master. Only you can change your habits of a lifetime with the help of the Masters' grace. Things may appear worse, i.e., dreams, thoughts, feelings, but that is part of the undoing, part of the process. It is not to be misinterpreted in the way you are doing now. I can guide you, yes, but please show some courage and don't give up at every little thing that challenges you. "Have some guts!" Maharaj used to say to despondent, weak devotees. Make this day a good day! Take charge and live like *Brahman*, not like a frightened mouse! What are you afraid of anyway? Just ghosts! Nothing more!

Now I look forward to meditating

Q. I used to be very reluctant to meditate. I would clockwatch and impatiently wait for it to finish. I didn't think I was making any progress, so it was hard to keep going. However, now things have changed. I look forward to meditating because it has become a very peaceful and joyful experience. Now I no longer check the clock and it is like I can't get enough of it!

A. Great to hear that your determination and practice are paying off. Now there is a natural urge to meditate for far longer periods. This is wonderful! This peace and joy that has begun to flow freely is what Maharaj calls "the fragrance of Selfless Self". So, keep going, keep going!

News of liberation

Q. I was introduced to the work of Ramana Maharshi and Nisargadatta a decade ago. Since then, I have felt attracted to these teachings, although I admit I have not practiced *Atma Vichara*, (Self-enquiry), enough. I met Shri Ramakant Maharaj a few days ago via videos. His way of communicating has encouraged me to return to a meditation practice. I am interested in receiving the *Naam Mantra*. If you need more information about me, please don't hesitate to ask.

A. I suggest you read Maharaj's book *El Ser Sin Ser* first. Once you have more of an understanding of his teachings, then we will see about the *Naam Mantra*.

Now I would like to offer you some encouragement. You may sometimes wonder if anyone has been liberated from their small selves after following for some time the practice, like you, do? The answer is, yes! Occasionally, I hear from seekers, after a long period of silence. These communications are different because they do not contain any questions and not only that, they are very uplifting because they convey the news of liberation with expressions of gratitude. Here are a couple of examples:

"I did not write to you for more than a year, after one day that profoundly changed my life, as I wanted to make sure the state was permanent! On that day, I came home from work, worried about a financial matter and after eating, I began to read for a while, as usual, from the book, *Selfless Self.* While I was reading, suddenly all the worry and tension disappeared and I was certain that I am the silent and transparent Presence, that never changes and has always been there. I am before this body and before everything. And that will never disappear! There is no reason to analyze that moment. It is difficult to explain, except to say that, the deep feeling of tranquillity has not been lost. The brain continues to create thoughts but they are more diffuse and remain outside a space of silence, like traffic noise.

Some thoughts make themselves heard louder, but there is always the security of that Presence in the background. And since that day, I have also understood some things that I read in the book *I am That,* such as "a state that cannot be expressed in words but can be experienced" and many others. I also know that after so many years of reading and spiritual practices, the Ultimate Truth which has always been there has found me and there is nothing more to learn… just to live it now, which has been happening since then. I will always express huge gratitude to you for spreading the wonderful teachings of Shri Ramakant Maharaj and the Inchegiri Navnath Sampradaya.

The second one comes from someone who had indicated last year that the Conviction was established. She had entered a quiet space. Recently, she contacted me saying: "I am writing to say hello and express to you my love and gratitude. Always in silence and emptiness! No questions, no ups and downs. Conviction is ever present, love and blessings". I have quoted only two examples here but I know of others who have reached the destination. There are those who have Conviction but choose to remain quiet and don't make contact. That was a little encouragement to spur you on!

Q. What, if anything, did Maharaj say regarding Kundalini Awakening and completion? Am I on the right track that he would not give it much of any importance because it is just phenomenon and body knowledge?

A. You're right! Maharaj was quite disparaging in a humorous kind of way about this kind of talk. He would often say "this chakra, that chakra, this chakra, Kundalini, forget it all!

Q. I was in the ashram of Nashik in 2018 and received the *Naam Mantra* from the Master, Ramakant Maharaj, some months before he passed away. The Advaita Vedanta community in Spain is really small, almost negligible. I guess that in big cities like Madrid or Barcelona, there are more people, who at least, have heard about it? But in the very south of my country where I live, I think I must be the only one. By the way, could you tell me if there is any active ashram in Europe? We could do with one to bring us all together.

A. It's a good idea! An active ashram in Europe sounds like a wonderful idea. Ideas such as these have been many, whereas implementing them is a different story! Who is going to initiate the project? I am sure there would be a lot of interest, but for that, we need volunteers and resources. Would you like to initiate this project? It would be great!

Not surprisingly, I never heard from the seeker again, since encountering Maharaj ten years ago. Unfortunately, I can count the number of devotees who have offered to do some kind of *seva*. If someone else does the work, then others will be interested and get involved. The idea is still a good one. Needless to say, communicating online does not compare to having a physical building where we can meet, share, meditate and sing, etc. Maybe it will happen in the future, by the grace of Maharaj!

The Presence you are is already awakened

Q. If the person who wants to awaken is not the doer, then does that mean the person will never awaken, if Presence does not will it?

A. The answer to that is the Presence that you are is already awakened. The person is the illusion that is covering and obscuring your Presence, your reality, so it does not have anything to do with presence willing awakening or not willing awakening. The barrier is always your identification with the body mind. The only thing that is in the way of our awakening or Self-Realization, are all these layers of conditioning that have formed the persona, the pseudo self or self-image. Our goal is to erase them all and throw them in the dustbin.

The solution is easy if you follow it with discipline. Again, use dedication and determination. Use the Mantra and Self-enquiry. Absorb the knowledge and practice devotion to remove all the superimpositions that are covering your Presence. Once the ego has been thoroughly hammered and everything that is false and temporary has dissolved, then there will be liberation. And then, you will see that eternal state that you are, that you were, that you will be always.

Don't keep bad company!

Q. Maharaj talked about the importance of keeping the right company. Can you say more about that? I often considered this as in relation to people, eg., friends and family, but now I'm learning more and more about the danger of the "internal" tenants of the mind, ego and intellect.

A. Yes, it is important not to mix with negative energies, but equally important, not to listen to the continuous thoughts and ego talk. People, activities, negative thoughts, negative self-talk... all of it is bad company that will leave more and more impressions which you need to erase.

Q. From childhood, there has been fear and anger about being here in a body. I was told that I chose to be here, but I don't remember any such thing. It is heresay. When the 5 elemental body was produced and combined with vital breath and beingness, knowingness came about. There was no name before the body and even now, there is no name because it's all an overlay on "nothing". Is knowing ourselves as formless the end of the matter so that this "mishap" as Nisargadatta calls it, does not happen again?

A. Knowing ourselves as formless is the end, but that Conviction is spontaneous; it is not an intellectual conviction.

Q. I just finished reading *Selfless Self* and I also listened to the audio book on the YouTube channel, stopping at chapter 76. This book is amazing! It hammered the ego continuously, again and again. I was trying to switch attention to the invisible, formless, unidentified identity. Sometimes I stopped reading and meditated for a while. The ego almost dissolved. So far, no problem with the conviction. That is why I came to you. I really want to know the true reality.

A. It is good to hear about the effects which reading *Selfless Self* has had on you, but slow down! It is important to read very, very slowly, in order to absorb the knowledge. Your enthusiasm is great but there is no hurry. It is best to read one passage at a time and then meditate on it, dwell on it, turn it over, over and over. And yes, the audio book of *Selfless Self* will bring different teachings to your attention. It is also a good way of absorbing the teachings.

Q. I have been reading *Selfless Self* and now I have just finished *Who am I?* For me, they go together well. They are a perfect match. *Selfless Self* is very direct and straightforward, whereas *Who am I?* is different. Parts one to three explain some key concepts and the elaboration on them is simple and easy to understand. Part four to part six are very practical. After I spend some time practicing, I will read the book again and then I may have more understanding.

A. Good to hear! Both books are meant to be read many times. *Selfless Self* has a lot of power and many readers have said that when they read it, it feels as if Maharaj is talking directly to them. This is the effect of direct knowledge. There is a lot of repetition in this book, however, we need the hammering to remove all the layers of illusion we have accumulated over a lifetime.

Who am I? breaks down the teachings into a very simple language which makes them accessible to all. One need not know anything about Advaita Vedanta or nonduality before reading this book. It is a very practical manual that you can refer to again, again and again. So, keep reading slowly and absorbing.

Read *Timeless Years* as your story

Q. I have not read *Timeless Years with Shri Ramakant Maharaj* because I have a tendency to compare experiences.

A. I would encourage you to read it. The best way to read this book is for you not to read it as if it were the story and experiences of Charles and myself. Read it as your story. If you do it in this way, it will take you on the journey, travelling to Nashik and meeting Maharaj. Many who missed the opportunity of being with Maharaj feel that they can now meet him and get to know him through this book.

Step into my shoes and soon you will be with him. Also, those who have read it, tell me that the book had the effect of opening their hearts and increasing their devotion. And not only that, the book offers a unique perspective and deep insight into the Guru-disciple relationship.

Now, to finish, I would like to share a dream someone had a couple of months ago. He had read Nisargadatta's books. In his dream, all the Masters appeared including Ramana Maharshi. As the seeker looked surprised to see

Ramana there, Siddharameshwar smiled at him and pulled him up, saying, "Why are you surprised when we are all one? Then Ramakant Maharaj spoke: "Go and receive the *Naam Mantra* from Ann", followed by "Read Ann Shaw's book, *Who am I?*"

This seeker was naturally amazed. He got in touch with me and has since been initiated! This is a good example of how Maharaj is ever present, directing and guiding seekers to Truth. Have no doubt that Maharaj is here with us now, always. I was especially pleased to hear Maharaj's recommendation of the book *Who am I?* Maharaj had instructed me to write this book after the completion of *Selfless Self*. As with *Selfless Self*, he chose the book title, *Who am I?* Also, as before, he specified his wishes for simplicity as well as for a contemporary style, with the aim of reaching a mainstream audience.

As Maharaj attained *Mahasamadhi* in 2018, he never got to see the completed book, therefore, hearing his comment now, via the seeker's dream, was great! It was like an endorsement from the other side, so to speak.

There must be a longing for truth

Q. I sometimes think my *vasanas* are irredeemable.

A. All these questions and thoughts of yours are imagination at play, illusory. If everything is unreal, how can you talk about something being irredeemable? You are often looking for a way to delay enlightenment, i.e., saying if Self-Realization does not happen this time round, then maybe in the next incarnation...etc. While Self-Realization is attainable, you need to want it more than anything else in life! Without this deep urge, pining, longing for truth and self-involvement, it will not happen. So, how much do you really wish to be free of yourself and know your true nature?

Q. Just curious. the journey's end, is it near or some way to go still?

A. When you are established in your true nature 24/7 and nothing touches, upsets, bothers or wavers, when life is lived without cares or worries, when there is happiness and peace without cause all the time, then the journey has ended!

You feel the hurt because you have not yet dissolved

Q. As the practice progresses, does this awareness cause a reset in the flow of the illusion? It's as if by letting go of me, there are earthquakes in the illusion, both at work and at home with the family. At the moment, I feel like letting the hurt arise and trying to just let go. But how can I do that because if I say there is no me, then how can I feel someone has hurt me? We are after all, knowingly or not, the same oneness!

A. External things can change as you undergo the practice. There can be positive or negative energies at play – all illusion anyway. You can still feel the hurt because you have not yet dissolved. You can say there is no you, but that is just an intellectual statement. You are still very much here, so I suggest that you just let the feelings arise of hurt and anger or whatever else. As Maharaj says, these feelings, when expressed, are just noises. like barking dogs!

My desire to meet a woman persists

Q. I know *Brahman* will never allow it, especially at my age, but somehow, like a moth is attracted to a flame, my desire to meet a woman persists.

A. You have told me many times that Self-Realization is your only desire in life. So, why are you now once more running after an illusion, instead of continuing to uncover the reality within you? You know that "man" and "woman" are illusory concepts, related to the body form and not what we are in essence. Therefore, why give this illusion any attention? Maharaj says that when one is younger there are bodily needs and desires and you fulfil them. But when you are older, you should be turning within because you know you are not the body form.

Sometimes what happens during the cleansing process is that the same deep-seated thoughts, concepts, desires arise multiple times, until they are permanently removed. When this occurs, just let them arise and fall, appear and disappear. Don't feed them with your attention!

Forget the "how?" and the "why?"

Q. I feel as if I have just come alive in the last 2 years. Before that I had no interest in spirituality. Then suddenly, I started devouring book after book, till I found Ramakant Maharaj, and then you. Before I felt bored and empty, but now happiness is overflowing. How did all this happen and why?

A. Forget about the how and the why! Everything happens spontaneously. We are on this earth to fulfil one duty - Self-Realization! To wake up from the dream, to stop trying to find meaning and happiness from the illusory world. Be content and give thanks that your light is no longer dimmed, but shining bright!

We cannot dictate the speed of our journey

Q. A few years ago, I was much more driven to find the truth than I am now. Life has become more complicated. It feels like the fire that was pushing me forward has just gone out. That makes me both angry and sad.

A. The fire has not been extinguished. What has happened is that you have had to turn your attention to other pressing matters which are demanding most of your time and energy. Don't be angry or sad! You know that this situation is temporary. When it passes, the drive will not only pick up again but be even stronger. We cannot dictate the speed of our journey. Know that I keep you in my prayers always. Rest assured that all will be well!

Remind yourself that the family is an illusion, too

Q. I am going through a very difficult time, even though I know that everything is an illusion. All I can do just now is try to be the best husband and father I can be. I am committed to the family.

A. Sometimes due to difficult circumstances and pressures, life becomes more intolerable and one desperately needs to hold on tightly to something, to feel less alone and ease the heavy burden. When this happens, it is normal to need greater support and to cling to something or someone. Of course, it is important to look after your family, but your primary commitment should be to Self-Realization. While going through this difficult patch, it is important to remind yourself from time to time, that everything is an illusion, including your family!

Who is lonely?

Q. I am still hoping that my wife will show more interest in these teachings. If she did, the daily pressure would be less. It would be wonderful if we could do the practice together and journey together.

A. Some devotees find the practice a lonely road, so they wish to bring their partners or friends along with them even when they are clearly not interested in spirituality. Stop hoping this will happen as it takes your attention outwards instead of within! And besides, this recurrent thought keeps perpetuating the illusion that you are a separate individual who is weak and lonely. Who is lonely? When the going gets tough, that's when you need to be strong and not look for anyone else to hold your hand.

I'm not interested in devotion

Q. When I read *I am That*, Nisargadatta did not talk about devotion. It was all about knowledge. Nisargadatta wasn't devotional, was he? But his disciple Ramakant talks about it a lot. I want the knowledge but I'm not interested in devotion?

A. The book *I am That* was written primarily for Westerners. With that in mind, Maurice Frydman omitted the subject of devotion from this book, so as not to alienate western readers. To say that Nisargadatta Maharaj was not devotional is completely untrue. You only have to look at his earlier books, to see this or observe footage of him doing *puja* to his Master, Shri Siddharameshwar, and singing the *bhajans* four times a day. Nisargadatta said many times that without his Master, Shri Siddharameshwar, Self-realization would not have occurred.

Many followers of Nisargadatta Maharaj have only read *I am That* and yet, Nisargadatta himself, later on stated, that as his understanding had evolved, what had been conveyed in *I am That* was not the final truth. There were also very few references in *I am That* to the "Inchegiri Navnath Sampradaya", the great Lineage of which he was a part. This lineage is a very humble lineage where respect and devotion to one's Master is highly revered, along with the recognition that without the Master, Self-Realization would not have taken place. The spontaneous gratitude for the Guru or Master is a central thread that runs through the whole lineage.

Presence is not limited by space

Q. I know of someone who paid an extortionate amount of money to sit close to a famous spiritual teacher in the West. He did this so as he could connect and absorb the teacher's high vibrations.

A. This is nonsense! If a teacher is Self-Realized then his Presence, the energy that is emitted is not limited by space. The omnipresence is felt all around him. Your friend is misinformed. He must think that the Presence is contained in the teacher's body. And also, here the teacher is accountable for exploitation, for charging extra for the illusory privilege of being seated next to him!

Q. I have been reading the *Upanishads* and also looking at Michael James videos.

A. You are roaming again! Just continue clearing out your hard drive, instead of wasting energy trying to work out various concepts, such as who says what. etc. Stay with no-thing! All this is just more entertainment for the mind – noise, when what's really needed is stillness and quiet.

Burning Desire for Truth

Q. Some seekers awaken after a short time and yet for others, it may take years? There does not seem to be any logical explanation for this!

A. The most important ingredient for Self-Realization is an unceasing passion and drive to find out who or what you are! Some seekers have a strong drive at the beginning of their journey, but shortly after, when they are faced with life's challenges, their determination weakens and just peters out. For others, even though they may know they are merely illusory, conditioned constructions, the fear that arises in the face of being demolished feels so uncomfortably real, all-consuming and intolerable that they give up at that point. There must be a fire within that is burning, longing to know the truth of your existence. Keep the fire burning until Spontaneous Conviction arises!

Maharaj's dismissal of all concepts is so refreshing

Q. What I find so refreshing and helpful about Maharaj's teachings is his dismissal of all concepts. I used to spend so much time and energy trying to grasp the words teachers use to communicate, trying to understand the truth intellectually. Now I know this is not the way.

A. Yes! You are prior to language, prior to all words and concepts. Intellectual knowledge to stimulate the mind keeps us on the merry-go-round of the search, as we analyze the words, attempt to grasp their meanings, and delude ourselves into believing that we have "got it"! Granted we must start off with intellectual understanding, but then, the knowledge needs to be absorbed, so that there is no separation between being and knowing.

Meditate where and when you can

Q. Is meditation only beneficial if the environment and posture are perfect?

A. Believing that meditation is only beneficial if you have the ideal environment and perfect posture is an illusion. It is also the way the mind tricks you into making excuses for not doing the meditation. Forget about perfection! Meditate where you can and when you can!

Q. We are not to analyze what the Master's say (don't take words literally), why not?

A. The Master is speaking from the Source. He is not speaking from the mind. Whatever the Master says is truth and therefore, not to be analyzed by the mind. Instead, you are to accept what he says without the mind. The Master has to use words to convey Truth, but you are to listen to, and hear, the meaning behind the words, that are generated by the power coming from Source.

Q. What did Maharaj mean by the "two thorns"?

A. We have been conditioned by the illusory world, society, family, teachers, etc. We call this programming and influencing of wrong knowledge that we have been subjected to, the thorn of illusion. When we listen to "right knowledge" and uncover the reality of our existence, we use this secondary thorn to remove the primary thorn. And at the end of our journey, we throw both thorns away.

Q. I feel I am almost merging with the infinite?

A. Who is almost merging? You are the infinite, have always been the infinite and will always be That! Drop the "I" and you are That.

Q. I don't feel the meditation is bringing me any peace.

A. Peace is already there. You are peace itself. It is the "I" that is in the way. Turn your attention away from the illusory "I" and bring it to your Eternal Presence.

Surrender

Q. How do we become honest with ourselves to the point the surrender become real?

A. When knowledge turns into Conviction that is when it becomes Self-Knowledge. What this means is that the knowledge that you are not the body is being absorbed. And this gradual and growing knowingness of your reality, your divinity, simultaneously grows with an awareness of your Self-transformation.

The dynamics and momentum of this Self-transformation that bring up deep experiences of love, joy and peace, spontaneously spur you on more consciously to surrender honestly and totally. You have a taste and it is natural and spontaneous to want more! In other words, as the Conviction deepens, what used to be merely intellectual knowledge is now grounded in the core of your being. In other words, it feels real. Why does it feel real now? Because knowing and being have merged and are one. You are the knower, the knowing – Jnani. I have tried to explain logically what is not a logical process ... but you will taste the flavour behind these words.

The hollowness of Neo-Advaita

Q. What about Neo-Advaita which has become very popular?

A. Ah! Neo-Advaita! I can say quite a lot about that! Unfortunately, these days, many seekers get caught up in the Satsang circus of Neo-Advaita. There are Teachers to be found all over the world, claiming to have woken up - some of them with thousands of followers - and others with millions, advertising themselves as Self-Realized beings! Living as we do today in such a fast-paced world, it is not surprising that the "Neo-Advaitin Movement" which sells fast enlightenment is so popular!

The precept "Know Thyself" going back to the time of the ancient Greek thinkers in the 5th century, has always been a serious pursuit involving self-introspection, focus, concentration. Above all, this pursuit was time-consuming, as well as requiring dedication and patience! The search for truth is a noble and respected one. It was never a fast quest and can never be, no matter what age we live in!

While Neo-Advaita shares the same essential truth as classical Advaita Vedanta that, "We are already free and liberated", that is where the similarity ends. Advaita Vedanta has always employed a methodology to guide students from duality to non-duality. It uses a proven method that works, namely, the three stages described as *Shravan* (adequate hearing), *Manana* (constant remembrance) and *Nidhidhyasana* (contemplation or meditation) Or Listening, Reflection and Steady Contemplation or Integration. The first stage means 'hearing'. ... But it is not enough to simply hear the teaching. Reflecting on it is necessary to enable its absorption. And thirdly, there needs to be Steady Contemplation or Integration. This three-stage process is systematic. You cannot skip over any one stage, but follow them in sequential order.

There are different paths to Self-Realization and they all require lengthy periods of *sadhana* to purify the mind and remove the ego. We cannot skip this basic step. If we do not cleanse the mind, if we do not even begin the process of Self-enquiry, then how can we possibly wake up and become enlightened!

We have fast food, fast cars and a fast life, so Neo-Advaita comes along and purports to offer us fast Enlightenment to fit our busy lifestyle! It sounds ideal! If only it were that easy! If only it were true! Yes! we must move with the times, but when it comes to waking up or Self-Realization, there is no such thing as "Fast Self-Realization".

Neo-Advaitin teachers will tell their followers: "Realize that you are already free, eternal, omnipresent, etc. There is only now! Enjoy your life to the full!" And so, their eager listeners take it all on board, believe what they hear, and then count themselves as one of the enlightened! Unfortunately, though, this kind of talk is nothing but hot air – nothing more than hollow words, illusory concepts!

Carried along by sheer enthusiasm, both the teachers and their followers really seem to believe they are liberated! But that belief is skin deep and for want of a kinder word, it is delusional! They are kidding themselves on! Liberation does not happen to a person. Liberation means freedom from the person. The Neos who claim to be liberated still have their old identities intact. Nothing has changed. They are still body-minds, functioning from their still fully present egos!

So, while they may spout out words of oneness, love and freedom, nothing has intrinsically changed in them. They remain just as they were before encountering Neo-Advaita. They remain egos. All that has changed is that the ego now indulges in a lovely new thought of "I am enlightened"!

So, what is the conclusion? There can be no such thing as awakening or enlightenment without preparation, *sadhana*, or a process of undoing the ego and removing the illusory layers. Self-transformation can only take place by turning within, just like those in ancient days did during their noble search to "Know Thyself".

It is easy to understand how many in today's world are attracted to Neo-Advaita, yet, what is the point, if it does not lead to Self-transformation and Self-Realization!

So, we have established that there is no such thing as "Fast Enlightenment" or "Fast Self-Realization". Fortunately, though, the Masters of our Lineage offer us a shortcut. Thanks to the sacrifices these Masters made, the years they spent in self-exploration and deep meditation, we now have clear instructions, that will slowly but surely, lead us to the destination of Self-Realization! The Masters don't just talk about our true nature, they show us how to uncover it. They don't just say, like the Neo-Advaitins, "You are already liberated!" They will say, "You are already liberated, but you do not know that you are". And then, they will show you ways of removing the illusory layers, the barriers that stop you from knowing yourself!

We have been given clear instructions for our practice and various tools to help us with the demolition of the ego. The lineage teachings are above all pragmatic and direct. We don't have to believe in anything. Self-Realization means liberation from the little self, it means being free from the pseudo I, the mind, the ego. The process of undoing using Self-Enquiry, Mantra, meditation and devotion guarantees that when Enlightenment or Self-Realization spontaneously happens, it will not be a delusion or a concept, but rather, the realization of our eternal Reality!

Part Two: Q & A's on Advaita Vedanta/Non-Duality & the Lineage Teachings

To come across the "Inchegiri Navnath Sampradaya Lineage" and its great Masters is indeed auspicious! These pragmatic teachings are solid and complete. And when they are followed with discipline, results are guaranteed! Nisargadatta Maharaj said, "I am not making you a disciple, I am making you a Master!" Ramakant Maharaj said the same thing.

It is so important to be guided by authentic teachers who can guide seekers, slowly, but surely. Those who have undergone the same process and have firsthand, direct experience are the best qualified!

Q. What is the difference between Advaita Vedanta or Non-Duality, and the Lineage Teachings?

A. There is no difference where the Knowledge is concerned. The Teachings of Advaita Vedanta - Non-Duality are the same as the Lineage Teachings. But there are some additions in the Lineage, other tools that complement the process, that will take us to our destination – such as the *Naam Mantra*. There is also a richness to be found in the Lineage teachings and practice, such as Devotion to the Guru/Master, *Bhajan* singing, etc.

Advaita Vedanta by itself can sometimes appear dry, whereas, if we are fortunate to be with a Master and practice devotion and worship, it will bring the whole process to life! The humility exemplified by the Masters keeps us humble, too. And if we surrender to them, the ego is chopped into little pieces much faster!

Advaita Vedanta can sometimes come across as overly intellectual. In Advaita Vedanta, the Teacher is respected and revered, whereas in the Lineage, the relationship between the Guru and the disciple goes much deeper. This intense relationship can quicken the process. The intimacy forged between the Guru and the disciple means that a deep connection is established at the heart level. The disciple's love for the Guru is profound and lasting because the Guru is responsible for showing him his true identity. That depth of love does not suddenly disappear when the Guru leaves the body, but continues as devotion. For many, the practice of Advaita Vedanta ends with Liberation, whereas in the Lineage, Liberation is followed by Devotion.

Maurice Frydman in the Appendix of Nisargadatta's classic, *I am That,* said: "The teaching of the Nath Sampradaya offers the seeker the royal road to liberation, a road in which all the four by-lanes of *bhakti, jnana, karma* and *dhyana* seem to unite. ... the path shown by the Nath sect is the best of all and it leads direct to liberation".

Use discrimination when searching for a Master

Q. How does one know if a Master is realized?

A. We know because of the energy around the Master. If there's peace, calm and happiness emanating from the Master, and if you are mature, it is easy to recognize a

Master. Unfortunately, younger seekers are unable to discriminate and sometimes, will often end up in the company of power mongers instead. I'll give you an example: when I was in Nashik Ashram with Ramakant Maharaj, once there was a group of devotees there and they were asking the same questions, to Maharaj: "Are you realized? How do we know you're realized?" And Maharaj was kind of frustrated. "Why are you asking such a silly question? Find out if you are realized!" he responded. At that point, I said, "The devotee knows because there's a resonance with the Guru and you can immediately see it, feel it. You know." At this point, Maharaj turned his head towards me and fixated for a few minutes. He smiled, pleased that my comment had dissolved the silly questions.

Don't identify with the lineage

Q. Does one have to belong to the Lineage of the Inchegiri Navnath Sampradaya to receive the *Naam Mantra*?

A. There's no such thing as belonging to the lineage or joining the lineage, but at the same time, there has to be respect for the lineage. When you receive the *Naam Mantra*, it's not like, eg., "Transcendental Meditation" which is like a Mantra that's on its own, a standalone mantra! Some people have come to me, saying, "can I get the *Naam Mantra* because I've tried TM and now, I want to try the *Naam*". While there's no formal joining of the lineage, when you take the *Naam Mantra*, you must have respect for the lineage Masters. When you receive the *Naam Mantra*, there takes place an automatic link between yourself and the Masters. And that link is very strong. It is eternal and protective. When, with sincerity from the heart, you receive the Mantra, you will be linked to the Masters for eternity. They will protect you throughout life and be there for you when you leave the body. I experienced this blessing with my late husband! Such grace! It was immense and beautiful.

While we respect the lineage, at the same time, we're not joining any kind of organization. That would be a concept, and as you know, Maharaj was very clear about the knowledge shared by the lineage. He saw that some devotees like to identify with the lineage and yet this knowledge does not belong to the Inchegiri Navnath Sampradaya. If you take on a new identity such as the lineage, then you're back in the illusion. This knowledge is universal Knowledge - for everyone!

Don't let the spiritual ego take over

Q. I still feel very attached to my family. They don't share these teachings. Do I have to choose between the family or follow the teachings?

A. Attachment to anything, needs some attention to reduce it and let it go, in order to realize that the family is part of the illusion. Your duty to your family comes first. If you ignore the family duties, then that is the spiritual ego taking over which is not the way. This is a householder lineage which means that looking after the family and following the lineage teachings are not incompatible. Most of the Masters did so. They are our examples.

Q. How can I bring the lineage *sadhana* into my work life?

A. This lineage is a householder lineage...Shri Bhausaheb, Shri Siddharameshwar, Shri Nisargadatta, Shri Ramakant Maharaj were all married, working and with families. They are wonderful examples of combining work, family life and spiritual life. They saw these different elements in life, as challenges to be overcome, that would deepen their total faith in the path, in Truth.

Who is currently following the steps of Maharaj

Q. I wanted to ask you if there is any member of Master Siddharameshwar Maharaj's family, who teaches in India or who is following the steps of the Great Master? Or is there anyone in Nashik Ashram who holds the teachings after Master Shri Ramakant left the human body?

A. There was the beautiful grandson of Siddharameshwar Maharaj called Balwant Maharaj. Unfortunately, he caught Covid 19 and left the body around two years ago. I met him a few times. His company was blissful! Currently, there is no one at the ashram in Nashik. What usually happens is that there is a gap between the Masters, until suddenly, and spontaneously, the next one arises.

Chidananda – Advaita in a nutshell

Q. I love the *bhajan Chidananda* and the text is wonderful – pure Advaita! Where does this *bhajan* come from?

A. It is beautiful and really, it contains the whole teachings in a nutshell, using the *neti neti* approach ("not this, not that"). We are reminded that we are not the body, not the mind, not this, not that. That we are no thing. It was written by Adi Shankaracharya, the great Hindu philosopher, Advaitic scholar and revered saint. He summarized the non-dualistic philosophy in just six stanzas. His remarkable, impromptu composition encapsulated the essence of Advaita philosophy in its entirety. "There is nothing but Atma, the True Self, complete peace, freedom and joy. I am that Eternal knowing and Bliss, Shiva. love and pure consciousness".

Q. Are the teachings of the lineage the same as Advaita Vedanta?

A. The teachings and process of this lineage are the same as Advaita Vedanta. First of all, we are taught that everything we see is illusion. We need to Self-enquire and find out what we are not, using the *neti neti* approach. This means dissolving all the concepts and attachments. After that, we are taught that everything is *Brahman* – Reality. Once this knowledge is absorbed, the Spontaneous Conviction arises which then brings about a shift. After that, everything is seen from the perspective of *Brahman*, instead of from that of the former ego-mind.

No correlation between spirituality and sex

Q. The Master, Shri Siddharameshwar, says there is no correlation between spirituality and sex, that one can live a normal sexual life, but with detachment, and also have children. Nisargadatta, I think I heard him say that disinterest in sex is a consequence of our spiritual practice and not an imposition to achieve realization or speed up the process. Many wise men in the past had families. But I saw an interview of a direct student of Shree Ganapatrao Maharaj who talked about *Brahmacharya*. I was also reading from different sources that sex was only contemplated for procreation and not for the pleasure derived from it – that it should be avoided for other reasons. Many Swamis like Sivananda or Anandamay Mai Ma, Ramana Maharshi himself and other saints gave great importance to *Brahmacharya*. Anandamay Mai Ma for example, did not allow her husband to touch her ever in her life.

It's not a big deal. Let's say that at the moment, I am indifferent to sexual activities, but my wife is not. So, there is conflict. Should I leave my family and go and live isolated in the mountains and in some ashram? But the thought of abandoning them is too painful. I am faced with a dilemma.

A. Don't get caught up in rules... the do's and don't's. And stick with the examples of the great Masters of the Lineage! It is a householder lineage where most of the Lineage Masters were married with children. Some like Shri Ranjit and Shri Ganapatrao were not married.

Shri Siddharameshwar taught that, alongside detachment, a normal sexual life is possible. Shri Ramakant Maharaj also taught that, as one goes deeper into Self-Knowledge, and knows himself more and more to be the Reality, and not the illusion of the body, then desires for material and pleasurable things, including interest in sex, lessens spontaneously. Therefore, whatever transpires regarding sex and other desires is a consequence of the practice and not a rule!

Needless to say, a householder lineage in India is not the same as one in the West. In India, traditionally speaking, (though changes are afoot), the role of the wife is clear - it is one of duty and service to the husband and family: to attend to the chores at home, have children, and where necessary, look after and support her husband in his spiritual practice, by respecting his need for privacy and time! And if there is a Guru/spiritual Master, the wife's role of service and duty to the husband who is now, say, a *Jnani* is even greater! Look at the way Shri Ramakant Maharaj's wife, Anvita, (herself also a longstanding disciple of Nisargadatta Maharaj), has served Maharaj over the years! Her devotion is exemplary! The reverence, bowing, service, all of it!

Now, in the West, women are not going to behave in this way in a marriage, are they? Therefore, culturally, it is not surprising that there may be some conflict or friction if the couple do not share a "spiritual life". To return to your question: "Should you leave your wife and family because of your indifference towards sex and the seeming conflict with your wife? Absolutely not! The mind is playing tricks with you! I need to remind you that you are in the middle of the process of undoing all the illusory layers. And what you are experiencing just now is simply a moment of turbulence. Be assured that it will pass! When the process is finally completed, it will bring about a shift. And from that fresh perspective, all the current conflicts will dissolve.

When you absorb the knowledge that you are not the body, with detachment, you will be able to witness the body functioning in the world, playing different roles, and that includes sex! So, there is no problem. Don't give it too much attention, otherwise you will make it a problem.

When the Reality of your true nature is established, then nothing will upset you. But at this stage of your practice, a lot of things will keep surfacing, so, be alert and avoid the mind traps! The whole point of the cleansing process is to purify and clear the space so that Ultimate Truth can emerge. So, take heart! I assure you that when your foundations are solid, all these feelings and mental activity will cease. And by that time, even if, say, a cyclone hit you, there would be no effect, since what you are is impenetrable. Trust the Masters and trust the practice. Keep going forward with courage. You are undergoing self-transformation. All will be well!

Universal knowledge

Q. When Maharaj spoke about the knowledge shared by the Lineage Masters not belonging to the Lineage, what did he mean?

A. What Maharaj is saying is that the knowledge shared by the Lineage Masters is not their property. It is universal knowledge to be shared with everyone. Here we are also reminded that any kind of identification keeps us in illusion and that includes identification with the Lineage!

Q. Does the *Guru Shishya* relationship transcend death irrespective of whether I gain liberation in this life or not? I mean does it continue beyond this life and into eternity?

A. Of course!

Jnani dimension

Q. Master Bhausaheb is near me often. I'm deeply grateful for his grace. Thanks for sharing your experience with our Guru. He is near you, obviously. You know I used to be Buddhist and was very involved with *bodhisattvas*, especially Padmasambhava and Avalokiteshvara. I'm beginning to think that the Masters of our lineage intervene often in the lives of devotees, just like the *bodhisattvas*! What a great blessing!

A. Of course their Presence is around us all the time! *Jnanis*, as you know, are completely liberated and they are with us always. They reside in a, let's call it, a '*Jnani* dimension' and they look after us. I have experienced this, many times. I have also heard numerous experiences from others where the Masters have made themselves known, often during difficult and challenging situations. It is a great blessing indeed! The lineage is very pure and ancient and the Masters' care for us is magnanimous!

Open your heart!

Q. The experiences I have during meditation are not very warm. In fact, I feel quite empty and cold.

A. The path of knowledge alone can be very dry. Open your heart! Increase your devotion. Re-establish contact with the Masters and ask them for guidance. The Mantra is not separate from the Masters but linked. Maintain your connection with myself and the lineage, otherwise the practice may feel dull and uninspiring.

Surrender

Q. As far as my problems go, I am finding that surrendering whatever transpires to *Brahman* is best. Everything is getting impinged on the one consciousness or Brahman. While the *Naam Mantra* will remove the impurities that cloud my true nature as *Brahman*, surrender stemming out of a sense of helplessness, will keep me sane moment by moment.

A. Yes! As I said, find what works for you. Surrendering out of a sense of helplessness is powerful. You can also surrender out of pure devotion for the love of Sadguru, be that Ramana or Ramakant? You have had a lifelong devotion to Ramana, so that should help the surrendering too..."not my will, but thy will be done"!

Book Reading

Q. Should I stop reading books by teachers other than the Lineage teachers?

A. I would say that when you're freshly initiated, read only the most direct teachings. Each Lineage Master advances the teachings further, refines them and makes them more direct and simple. So, why read other books by other teachers? Ramakant Maharaj is the most direct, so stay with him. With meditation practice, your reading days will quickly come to an end. As Maharaj says, better to turn within and read your own book. This means look inside and find out who you are.

Q. Should we read the *Dasbodh*?

A. All the Masters recommend it. I would say it was written at a certain time, for a certain age. Some of it sounds quite antiquated nowadays. However, there are a lot of gems to be found, therefore, it is worth dipping into from time to time.

Q. I have started reading your book *Timeless Years*. I feel that I am with Maharaj, that I am on the journey you went on.

A. Yes! I have heard this said many times. When you read *Timeless Years,* you're supposed to read it as your story and not as the story about Charles and myself. For those who missed meeting Maharaj in the flesh, so to speak, this book enables a meeting and communion with the Master. You will get to know Maharaj through the book. Many devotees have told me also that it opens one's heart for devotion. I would say it is a very good vehicle for devotion.

Q. Yes! I'm finding that. It is really true. It is a real treasure for me to read it and I I thank you for bringing this out. It's definitely unique, wonderful and touching, very deeply touching, amazing.

A. It's also a kind of an insider view of the Guru-disciple relationship and how the transformation of the devotee occurs by becoming one with the Guru.

Clear all doubts before Initiation

Q. I had such a wonderful experience of connecting to deep Presence yesterday while reading the book *Be With You.* I had the day off and read it twice in the nourishing waters of a hot spring. I found that Maharaj came through very strong, awakening thoughtless reality. A deep thank you for your labour of love. I need more time to marinate, then I will contact you when we're ready for *Naam Mantra* Initiation.

A. Sounds like a lovely space yesterday. You're right! Take your time to prepare! There is no hurry. If you take things slowly, then the initiation itself will be all the more rewarding because you will feel ready. It is very, very important that you're absolutely sure that initiation is right for you. Don't go ahead if you have any doubts because these doubts will linger and then interfere with your practice.

Q. During an overnight shift, I was reading your book *Who am I?* when I suddenly felt no separation between myself, the words I was reading, and the one who wrote them. It was brief, but extremely clear and strong. Another thing that's been happening is that I seem to be internalizing the truth that "I am what I am looking for", more and more. There is a certain sense of safety to be found in this fact: I already am what I am looking for. I am also becoming more dispassionate about things in general, at least external things, since I already know that anything that can be experienced is non-self. You and Ramakant speak about all this, and I've understood it logically for a while now, but it seems to be sinking more deeply now. It seems like my acceptance of what I know to be true, (the teachings of the lineage), is growing exponentially, and a kind of relief and contentment accompanies it.

A. That is great to hear about your experience with *Who am I?* Maharaj used to say that one should not write spiritual books unless you are one with the knowledge and the reader because it is only in oneness, that the power of presence behind the words will be transmitted. Absorbing or internalizing the truth, that you are what you are seeking, plus growing in dispassion and accepting the teachings are very good examples of the progress you are making. And the contentment will continue to grow, as you go forward. Well done!

You are not on a race!

Q. I have finished reading both *Selfless Self* and *Ultimate Truth*. What next?

A. No next! Read them again and again. You are not reading novels! And you are not on a race! The knowledge in these books have come from the Source. It is living knowledge that is full of Presence. They have a lot of power. It is easy to read these books, but not so easy to absorb them. Read one passage at a time and then, dwell on it. That is the best way.

Meditation

Q. What does Maharaj mean by meditation? Sometimes he is referring to Mantra meditation and at other times, to meditation? Please explain!

A. With Mantra meditation as you know, we are reciting the *Naam* with full concentration. We are focussing on that! That is all we're doing. At other times, when Maharaj uses the word meditation, he is referring to a practice further on down the road. At the secondary stage, when you're a little more advanced and established, the meditation Maharaj talks about is a constant dwelling in Source 24/7. You are staying with Selfless Self all the time. The more you practice, the more effortless it becomes. The aim is that, eventually, with practice you won't have to make any efforts to dwell in your Source. It will happen, spontaneously, and it will continue like that all the time, without any effort. That is what Maharaj means by meditation. True meditation is just being as you are - your true nature effortlessly.

Q. Master Shri Bhausaheb Maharaj meditated from 12-18 hours for more than 15 years. How can we achieve realization with only two hours a day meditation?

A. In Bhausaheb Maharaj's day, the main practice was *Nama Yoga*. Most of his disciples came from the countryside. They were generally uneducated, illiterate, and therefore, the practice that Bhausahaeb Maharaj offered them was simple *Naam Mantra* recitation. After him, we had Shri Siddharamehshawar Maharaj and the other Masters who quickened the practice and added other tools. For example, Siddharameshwar Maharaj emphasized employing discrimination and discernment. If you can separate what is illusion from what is reality, it will lead you in the right direction. And then, Nisargadatta Maharaj and Ramakant Maharaj came along, offering their very direct approaches. As each

Master conveyed their teachings in simple terms, we now have the whole package. Two hours a day is sufficient. We have the Mantra, we have Self-enquiry and we have the Knowledge. All we need is discipline and application and Self-Realization is achievable.

Sticky concepts

Q. During concentrated meditation, some memories from different periods of life, some information received during the day, or a few days ago come up. Can we say that such a thing means that the purification and removal of this incoming information takes place, so that things arise? That thoughts and memories from the past could be the way back?

A. The answer is yes! But sometimes because the memories are so deep and sticky, the same ones will come up again and again and again. I call these sticky concepts. While some memories and thoughts just come up once, followed by a clearance, others will be repetitive, resurface again and again, until finally they dissolve. Deeply held impressions need to be got rid of. We do not wish to keep or hold onto anything - good memories, bad memories, etc. Everything must be cleared out.

Naam Mantra

Q. I have only recently come across the *Naam Mantra*. What is it exactly?

A. In the Inchegiri Navnath Sampradaya Lineage, the *Naam Mantra* is given to sincere seekers. It is the same mantra which has been passed down from Master to Master, for more than a thousand years, going back to the time of Saint Dattatreya. This Mantra is not a stand-alone mantra, say, like TM – Transcendental Meditation, but one that is linked to the Masters. During Initiation with the *Naam Mantra*, the seeker should have complete faith in himself, the Master and the Mantra, to enable a transmission of power.

The Mantra is not given to those who already use a Mantra. Neither is it given to those who already follow a Master. You must stay faithful to one Master only.

During Initiation, those who receive the *Naam Mantra* promise to keep it a secret. The *Naam Mantra* is called the "Master Key" because it opens the door to Reality, to your Ultimate Truth. So, how does the *Naam Mantra* work? It is a meditation tool that hammers the ego and helps to remove the layers of illusion that are covering your true nature. In the same way that your sensitive spirit has been conditioned by parents, teachers, society, etc, the *Naam Mantra* now helps you with the process of deconditioning. It reminds you of your true identity. The meaning of the Mantra is *"I AM BRAHMAN, BRAHMAN I AM"*. The Mantra produces vibrations within, and through them, as you continue to recite the Mantra, you will come to know the Reality.

After concentrating on the *Naam Mantra* for some time, changes will take place. Gradually, all the illusory concepts and attachments that you identified with will dissolve and your true nature will begin to emerge.

A purification or cleansing process is needed to clear out everything that does not belong to your true nature, your real identity. It is needed to establish a strong foundation. As you recite the *Naam Mantra*, you are reminding yourself of your forgotten identity – that you are *Brahman*, *Paramatman*, the Source of everything. *Naam Mantra* meditation helps to absorb the knowledge, which in turn, leads to conviction.

Embed the *Naam Mantra* deep within you

Q. Do I need to concentrate on the meaning of the *Naam Mantra?*

A. In the beginning, it is important to just recite the Mantra continuously, automatically hammering the ego with your truth: *"I am Brahman, Brahman I am"*. You need not dwell on the meaning at the initial stage, just try to embed it deep within you. Later on, as the illusory layers begin to dissolve, you can contemplate on the meaning. But for now, just keep hammering, hammering the ego. After practising for some time, the *Naam Mantra* will continue reciting by itself, spontaneously, without your knowledge for 24 hours – while waking, dreaming, etc, all the time!

Demolish everything you think you are

Q. I have the conviction that I am not the body, that I am not my name. I can differentiate illusion from reality. At the same time, I know that everything is me, the consciousness that includes all kinds of matter and energy. I started to become aware of that after experiencing the feeling of Presence produced by being focused on the "I am" thought. Is the *Naam Mantra* somehow similar to this? Does it help to dissolve the fundamental concept (illusion), of being a separate entity ("I")? I am excited to hear about such a wonderful instrument, and I wonder if you could kindly elaborate on that?

A. In answer to your question "Does it help to dissolve the fundamental concept (illusion) of being a separate entity" Absolutely yes! It is invaluable. We are already realized - already our true nature, but that is obscured by layers of illusion, by the pseudo "I" and all its creations. We need to remove all that is obscuring our true nature. Self-realization means freedom or liberation from the small "i", the small self. The small, illusory "i" cannot co-exist with Ultimate Reality that you are. So, we need to demolish everything we think we are, all the constructs, the layers, impositions, etc.

The teachings and process of this Lineage are the same as classical Advaita Vedanta: first we are taught that everything we see is an illusion. We need to Self-enquire and find out what we are not, using the *neti neti* approach. This means dissolving all the concepts and attachments. After that, we are taught that everything is *Brahman*/Reality. Once this knowledge is absorbed, the Spontaneous Conviction arises which brings about a shift. And then, everything is seen from the perspective of *Brahman*, instead of from that of the former, "ego-mind".

How does the *Naam Mantra* assist us? The *Naam Mantra* is a powerful vibration. Its meaning is "*I am Brahman, Brahman I am*". When we recite the *Naam Mantra,* we are hammering the ego and displacing the illusory thought of "I am the body-mind". With practice, the constant repetition weakens the mind, until the "I am the body" notion is supplanted with the Truth of, "*I am Brahman*".

Regular spiritual practice is essential

Q. I often find it difficult to establish a regular routine with the practice. How critical is this for spiritual progress? Or is it different for everyone, depending on their circumstances?

A. Regular spiritual practice is essential for all. Like regular food for the body, we need regular practice, especially in the beginning, otherwise, we will continue to be drawn into the illusory world. Regular hammering has to take place. Regular disciplines all the time, especially in the beginning. What does "in the beginning" mean? It means at least for the first few months after receiving the *Naam Mantra*.

Experiences are transient and therefore illusory

Q. I have heard that some devotees have different kinds of experiences during meditation. I don't have any. Does that mean I am not performing meditation correctly?

A. Not at all! we should not compare ourselves to others. Some people have many experiences and some have very few. Some have none in the beginning, but they may come later on. Experiences can be helpful for showing us landmarks and giving us encouragement that we're on the right track, but having them, or not, does not imply that you're not performing your meditation correctly. After all, experiences are illusory.

Q. Can you tell me about the "signposts" devotees might experience and their importance/non-importance in knowing ourselves in a true sense?

A. Signposts such as visions of the Master, hearing his voice, feeling his touch give encouragement to devotees, offering reassurance that they are making progress. These signposts signify that the Master is pleased with their practice and he rewards the devotees by making his Presence felt in some way or other. Having wonderful light-filled experiences may be another signpost that the destination is near! So, the importance of these signposts, or landmarks as Maharaj calls them, is that they have the effect of lifting the Spirit and renewing one's efforts. Having said that, some devotees reach the destination without any obvious signposts. Either way, it is important to receive guidance and encouragement from the Guru! When we had what Maharaj called our "weekly reviews of Reality", and shared our experiences, Maharaj always said the same thing: "Very nice, very good, but it is not Ultimate Reality. Keep going. Go ahead! Go ahead!"

Guru means the remover of darkness or ignorance

Q. How important are spiritual visions and experiences?

A. When one is close to a Guru or Teacher, there can be visions of him or her, but then again, there might not be. There could be many or there could be few. Again, there are no rules. These do not happen because of the way we do our practice, they just happen, spontaneously, and that is why, when these questions and doubts arise, it is important to be guided by a teacher or guru. Guru means the remover of darkness or ignorance.

Charles and I were very fortunate to meet with Maharaj every week for what he called our weekly "revision of reality". It's important not to get stuck, not to have any doubts and not to think that you've ended the journey prematurely. When we met with Maharaj, he would ask us about our experiences that week and we would share them with him. Then Maharaj would just say, "Very good, but it's not ultimate truth! And really, it was the same every week. But it's good to check in with a teacher to make sure that you're not going down a blind alleyway while thinking you're doing great! Too many seekers grow impatient and delude themselves that the job is done, when they've only had one or two glimpses.

Q. After reciting the *Naam Mantra* and still within meditation, there arose from the darkness a golden light. Within that golden light were high frequency flashes of brilliance, sharply bright and then extinguished. It felt like a field of souls.

A. The golden light sounds lovely. We don't usually talk about souls in Advaita, as it suggests separation, when, in reality, we are one in essence.

Q. During the latter part of *Naam Mantra* meditation, there was a physical shaking of the body and a rapid speeding up of the Mantra. It felt as though, internally, there was a need to smash down the walls of illusion. This need was very pronounced when compared to previous meditations. This meditation was intense, with a tremendous will to break through. But at the same time, it felt that the intensity was down to a resistance in me not to see the truth.

A. The physical shaking and speeding up of the Mantra means that the vibration of the *Naam* is now working more strongly within you. Don't pay too much attention to the body shaking.

The ego is fighting for survival

Q. Namaste Mother, how are you? I hope always well. I am continuing, day after day, to follow the instructions of the Masters. I have noticed that my ego often gives me trouble. The mind does everything it can to take me away from the spiritual path and bring me back to worldly life.

It intensifies and presents me with non-existent problems, with recurring negative thoughts. It looks like a crazy monkey! In meditation, I often have spontaneous hand movements like *mudras* and circular movements of the pelvis in an anticlockwise spiral. I think Shri Ramakant Maharaj would say these are things that belong to the body. But the concentration when it happens tends to go towards these experiences, overshadowing the Guru Mantra. I have difficulty with discrimination. Do I have to continuously discriminate the five bodies or do I have to bring attention with discrimination every time the mind tends to move away from centre? I'm going through feelings of anger, depression, happiness and peace, like I'm on a roller coaster. With love and affection. I feel gratitude for you and the teachers for the great gift granted.

A. It is nice to be called mother! Thank you! It is very normal to be going through a mental and emotional whirlwind in the early days of reciting the mantra. It is a cleansing, a clearing out process, whereby everything is rising from deep within the subconscious, including memories, feelings, experiences, etc. That is the job of the Mantra, to bring things up and discard them. All you have to do is keep reciting. Ignore what is going on and trust that the Mantra is beginning to sweep everything away. I am not surprised the ego is causing you big trouble. That is because it does not wish to be crushed or annihilated. It is fighting for its survival! You say you're going through feelings of anger, depression, happiness, peace, etc. You can also do Self-enquiry. Ask yourself who is going through this? Who is happy? Who is depressed? etc. The answer, of course, is no one. These experiences are like the barking dog. Pay no heed! Focus on the *Naam* and ignore the rest, including the *mudras.* Another instruction: can you read English? If so, I would suggest my book, *Who am I?* which has a lot of guidelines and useful tips, as to how to manage the many different assaults from the illusory ego. But for now, persevere with your practice. It sounds as if it's going very, very well. Because of the roller coaster experience, just remember to keep your feet on the ground. The process is one of removing all the illusory layers, so that eventually, your true nature will be uncovered.

Devotion

Q. In the morning, before singing *Kakad Arati* and indeed, at various other times, first of all, I personally address, greet and show gratitude to the Master whom I consider my Guru, and then, I personally greet and bow to each of the other lineage Masters. According to some internal hierarchy, at the same time, when I bow to this or that image picture, I present the image of the Master and pronounce a Mantra. I do this with dedication. I am worshiping the one Essence, the principle, the Selfless Self just manifested through different forms.

The same applies when I prostrate before the Masters. Every day, when I wipe the images of the Masters, I kiss the feet of the Masters in the pictures, and I put my forehead to their feet and do the same with another, depending on the day of the week i.e., my Guru every day and other Masters alternately throughout the week in a circle. My question is: Is all this normal? Is it possible to do this? Isn't such an approach multi-worshipping?

A. Of course it's normal and it's also very beautiful. It shows a deep devotion to the Masters. We know that the images are many but there is only one Sadguru, and of course, it's not multi-worshipping, it is devotion, deep devotion. And the more devotion we can perform, the better, because each time we bow to the Masters a little more of the ego falls away. Therefore, keep bowing! But remember, that as we worship the Masters, what is really happening is we are worshiping Selfless Self, that which we are. There is no separation between the Masters and us.

Non-dual devotion

Q. In the lineage, we are encouraged to bow to the Masters. To me this is duality. How can it not be?

A. You see it as duality because you are coming from a body-based perspective. You are not separate from the Master. There is no difference between the two. And secondly, the Master is not a person. He is not the form. These Self-Realized Masters have transcended the body-mind. So, you are not bowing to a human being but to the Absolute. And this act of bowing to them deepens our Conviction that we are That, and subsequently, brings us closer to Self-Realization. When we bow to their divinity, we are bowing to that one same divinity in us.

Q. When I listen to the *bhajans*, immediately, I feel the presence of the Masters.

A. I have often heard this being said! It is not surprising in a way because the Masters sang these *bhajans* daily and continued to sing them till they left their bodies. There is a powerful energy emanating from the *bhajans* that comes from the strong link to the Masters who sang them, over and over again, for decades.

You are all three: worship, worshipper, worshipped

Q. About worship... I have always worshipped and continue to worship the Masters, their images and pictures. But I do it as something external, something separate, like there is a worshipper and there is some external object of worship that is separate from me. Lately, I have increasingly wanted to combine these external images together and worship the Unity - to bow to Selfless Self, the Presence, the Invisible Listener, through which all these external images are projected. I just want to bring everything to "one point" and bow to it, roughly speaking. But this does not, in the least, diminish my respect, love and devotion to the Masters.

A. At the early stage of the process, your devotion appeared to be in duality, as you worshipped and bowed to each Master separately, and one at a time. Now that your devotion is deepening, there is the recognition of the oneness of the Masters and the desire to bow to that Oneness. Remember that there is no difference between the Masters and yourself. There is no separation. When you bow to the Master, you are bowing to yourself, Selfless Self, the Presence within you, the Invisible Listener within you. Remember also that you are all three: the worship, the worshipper and the worshipped! You are all! This deepening of your devotion and the clarity it has brought, does not in the least diminish your respect, love and devotion to the Masters. On the contrary, this kind of one-pointed devotion will naturally increase your respect and love for the Masters because they have helped you to understand that unity or oneness. And as a result, you can express even more gratitude to them!

Devotion is acceptance of Reality

Q. How do I develop devotion? Devotion is something alien to the West?

A. It is your idea of devotion that is false. What is devotion? Devotion is acceptance of Reality, your Reality. When the knowledge has been absorbed and the illusory concepts removed, then Reality emerges. When Reality is accepted totally and completely as That which you are… that is the meaning of devotion. It is non-dual! It is not you worshipping something or someone external. There is nothing external. Everything is within you.

Were you an intellectual type prior to being?

Q. Devotion feels alien to me. I am an intellectual type!

A. I heard this same statement from someone else recently. I will respond to you in the same way: Were you an intellectual or any other kind of type prior to beingness? Of course, not! This is something you identify yourself with – it is a false and conditioned image you have of yourself. This concept of being an intellectual type needs to be thrown out along with the rest of them. It is part of the baggage that keeps your false identity functioning. Using the tools of Self-enquiry, discrimination and detachment, you will be able to drop everything you imagine yourself to be!

Always perform worship as if it were the first time

Q. My devotion and *puja* were more sincere in the beginning. Now I seem to be just going through the motions in a mechanical way. How to bring it alive again?

A. Open your heart and prepare your altar with love. Approach everything with a beautiful freshness, as if this were the very first time you were doing *puja*. You would not treat your loved ones in a mechanical way, therefore, why should you treat the Lord in such a way!

Q. As a Westerner, I find both devotion and the *bhajans* very alien.

A. "Devotion" appears to be an alien concept to westerners, like the *bhajans*, until we know there is no duality in devotion, and we understand that it is not a kind of holy, pious kind of expression to something other, but devotion to "Selfless Self". As Maharaj said many times: "There is no difference between the Master and the disciple. We are one."

First of all, understand that devotion means to be driven, to be earnest, having the determination to find out the truth of who/what you are. You are devoted to uncovering your inner Master. Secondly, when you accept the "outer" Master and surrender to him, he assists in guiding you to your inner Master. If everything is an illusion, then that includes the Master and the disciple. There is no Master and disciple, however, the process of accepting your Master, and surrendering to him, works in a magical or mystical, even alchemical way. The Master is a catalyst, a mirror in which you can see "Selfless Self". Also, when you trust the Master with full faith and accept him totally, humility grows. (In the book *Timeless Years*, I explain the process by saying, "Each time we bow to the Master, our egos become smaller.) Briefly, if we have full faith in the Master, in ourselves and in the *Naam Mantra*, then the Master's Presence rubs off on us and we become like him.

Self-Realization

Q. There are a number of teachers online who claim to be Self-realized. While listening to one of them, I began to feel unwell. The way he was talking and what he was saying made me feel bad, so, eventually, I turned him off.

A. If someone says he is realized, then he is not. What he is claiming is ego-talk. You need to use your discrimination rather than accept a teacher's claims. Being around or listening to an authentic Guru or teacher should always be a positive experience of peace, light, warmth – never a bad one! How do you know if a Guru is a true one? Because there will be resonance within you, a gut feeling - you just know! Develop more trust in yourself, then you will be able to discriminate between the true and the fakes.

Q. Does Self-Realization happen suddenly or gradually?

A. It is different for everyone, though it is more often than not, a gradual awakening. As the understanding deepens, there are more glimpses and insights, followed by pauses, more absorption, then maybe bigger insights, until nothing merges with nothing.

The body needs to catch up with Spirit

Q. Now, after meditation, the body often feels exhausted, and yet, when I first started meditating it was the opposite. I felt light and re-energised. I'm wondering what is going on?

A. As you go through the process of hammering the ego and removing the illusory layers, you are detaching yourself from all that you used to identify with, all that you thought you were, everything that made up your world. This process of undoing and letting go of a lifetime's baggage is demanding energetically. As the formless, unlimited nature is seen, and self-transformation is underway, put simply, the body is trying to catch up with Spirit. And sometimes the energy can feel excessively strong and overwhelming for the body, though it is not.

Q. How is it possible to be conscious of my divinity at all times?

A. The practices of Self-enquiry, meditation, absorbing the knowledge, singing the *bhajans* and remaining in your true nature as much as possible – all of these will lead to a deepening awareness of your divinity, 24/7. And with continuous hammering of the ego, your true, ultimate, divine nature will be established.

Devotion after liberation

Q. How can I ensure that Self-Realization will be permanent?

A. Number one, by undergoing a purification process. Number two, by continuing your devotion. The Lineage stresses the importance of devotion after liberation. Why? The Lineage is a Guru-centred one where the Masters make Masters of their disciples. After the disciple has been liberated, the devotion to his Master or Guru continues because there is the recognition, the fact that without the guidance of the Guru, his realization would not have unfolded. We have seen many examples of this in the Lineage, eg Shri Siddharameshwar's devotion to Shri Bhausaheb. Shri Ranjit and Shri Nisargadatta Maharaj's devotion to Shiri Siddharameshwar and Shri Ramakant Maharaj's devotion to Shri Nisargadatta Maharaj. Continued devotion to the Guru guarantees authentic and permanent Self-Realization.

The trap of causes we hold dear: one example – Being a Vegetarian

If we hold on to causes that are dear to us, we may jeopardize everything - our opportunity to be free from the illusory "I". All views, beliefs, causes, etc., are superimpositions on our Presence. There was nothing prior to the body-form and there will be nothing after the body-form expires. Here is a question, an interesting question from a seeker who has been preparing for Initiation, (to receive the sacred *Naam Mantra*), for some time. The subject revolves around him holding strong views about being a vegetarian. It could have been about any other cause that we hold dear: political, religious, etc. The cause is not important, but the illustration of how we sell ourselves to an illusory identity is! He asks the following:

Q. Dear Annji, a conflict has come up for me for proceeding with the *Naam Mantra* initiation. It arose when I saw this quote from Maharaj on a video. The quote is as follows: "Whether you take nonvegetarian or vegetarian food is not a concern. The way you are identifying yourself, that is what is most important". That Maharaj allows nonvegetarian food is a concern for me. I am vegetarian because I feel spirituality is also about nonviolence and not causing suffering to animals. This is hard for me since I feel the *Naam Mantra* would be a great help in awakening. Then he says, "I know God is leading me to the right Guru, and I am praying for the highest Guru to be revealed".

What we see here is that because of one quote that was not acceptable to this seeker's vegetarian views, he was about to throw everything out. Here it is very interesting to see how the mind is really playing tricks and how the seeker was running away from truth because his views on vegetarianism were challenged! I responded to him, and as I did, praying he would be able to keep his ears open and absorb what Maharaj was actually teaching.

I prayed that he would not just abandon the lineage and this wonderful opportunity for liberation, simply because of an illusory belief. Illusory maybe, but at the same time, it was a very, very strong one that was so challenging for him, he was about to forget about Initiation, the lineage and everything else. I responded in this way:

A. It is a shame that you quickly dismiss Maharaj, the lineage and the teachings because of a belief in vegetarianism. With respect, true spirituality is not about whether one is a vegetarian or not. The stances we take in this dream life are just that, stances, views, opinions preferences, beliefs. Vegetarian or non-vegetarian is one example, politics and philosophy are others. You say, "I feel strongly about this!" The whole point of the practice and the teachings is to dissolve this 'I' which is the pseudo "I", the created "I" that is responsible for developing these strong beliefs and lifestyles.

Maharaj and the lineage Masters teach from the stance of prior to beingness or prior to consciousness. It means that prior to the body mind there was nothing except the "Stateless State"! We knew nothing about vegetarianism or nonviolence or anything else. We learned these concepts with the manifestation of the body form. The purpose of the teachings is to stop identifying with the body form and all the illusory concepts we have acquired on route which have formed our identity.

The point of the practice is to remove everything you identify with, associate with, are attached to, such as those things that have created your self-image, including what is right or what is wrong. Suddenly, when you found this quote from Maharaj you felt threatened and decided that he is not the highest Guru. He cannot be because of his comments on vegetarianism. This is nonsense! You are acting from the body mind, from the perspective of someone who believes he is right, and even more right than Maharaj.

As I said, your strong views are part of your body mind identity. I understood that you wished to dissolve that, but now it doesn't sound like it, when it appears that you would rather hold onto your values that are body based, over and above those that are prior to the body mind - not to mention the highest teachings! Are you going to forfeit the opportunity for liberation because the ego, your mindset, won't budge? Are you going to say goodbye to Maharaj and the Lineage because you are bowing to your ego, instead of to Sadguru?

Please stop for a moment! Take time to contemplate what is going on! Maharaj's advice is correct: eat meat if you wish, don't, if you don't wish. Why is he saying this? Because the body has nothing to do with spirituality. The body and how we nourish it, does not affect the spirit. There are no rules in spirituality, in the real sense of the term.

As Maharaj says, spirituality is also an illusion. It is the secondary thorn that we use to remove the first thorn of illusion. And once it has served its purpose, we throw it away, we throw both thorns away. Your ego strongly reacted to this video, making you really believe that you know better than Maharaj. It is an ego trap that you cannot see! It shows an over righteous persona that feels attacked and threatened by truth and therefore, prefers to reject it. Would you rather remain as the illusory human being who is a vegetarian because you know it's right, rather than surrender that particular illusion and allow yourself to be the expansive self that you are - which is beyond all man-made beliefs, rules, dictates etc? Sadly, this knee-jerk response is lacking in both humility and an understanding of the teachings of the lineage. So, before you throw everything away, not for your own good, please take time to pause and reflect.

I was happy that he got back to me quickly before forfeiting a wonderful opportunity. He "got it" and responded with courage:

Q. I truly appreciate your clear explanation of Maharaj's understanding of this. I read that Ranjit Maharaj also was not particular about needing to be vegetarian. It does make sense that if everything is illusion or zero, as said by Maharaj and by Ranjit, then the compassionate Selfless Self or Paramatman would not place this restriction on awakening to the reality. And yes, it is "I" that is connecting to this view rather than reality. Yes, I see this stance as ego. I will keep an open mind and open heart. Your compassionate response touches me. More time is needed in being quiet and soul searching, in preparation for the sacred *Naam*.

The above is a good illustration of how we can get caught up very easily in principles and causes at a very high cost. Fortunately, this seeker realized in time that it was the ego that was resisting, and as a result, he was able to move on.

Q. Is it necessary to be a vegetarian to receive the *Naam Mantra*?

A. Why would it be, when what we eat is only connected to the food body and not to you. The one essential condition for receiving the *Naam* is sincerity and after receiving it, that you will not go looking elsewhere. Along with that, there is the promise not to divulge the sacred Mantra. If you do, it is a betrayal of trust. You betray your Master and you betray yourself and consequently, it renders the *Naam Mantra* useless. Maharaj sometimes initiated seekers freely, but when, if on occasion, he heard of it being abused and mistreated he held back and became more discriminating about giving the Mantra to seekers.

If the mind body is impure is it not blasphemy?

Q. What is the difference between the *Naam Mantra* and reciting another mantra or Divine name? And if the mind body is impure, is it not blasphemous to recite God's name?

A. Our reality is prior to and beyond all names. The *Naam Mantra* is ancient and dates back to the time of St Dattatreya, over a thousand years ago. The Lord's names or Divine names for God are manifestations of *Brahman*, the Absolute, the unchanging, Ultimate Reality. How can reciting the *Naam Mantra* or any other mantra, be seen as blasphemous, when what we are reciting is our true identity, our true nature – "*I am Brahman, Brahman I am*" is our truth.

Don't confuse the body mind with our reality, our spirit. The body mind is an illusion. What you are in reality, under all the layers of superimpositions is *Brahman*, and *Brahman* has never been affected by your body mind. *Brahman* has never ever been touched by anything, by so-called impurities. *Brahman* is separate. If you wish, at times, to utter the name of the Lord, then do so. If you're drawn to a particular Deity, then aspire. but remember that, ultimately, what we are is nameless.

Regarding the efficacy of the *Naam Mantra,* the sacred *Naam* is ancient and has been empowered by the great Masters who have spent lifetimes in meditation. The *Naam Mantra* works as a vibration which has the power to transform the body mind. It is a very potent tool that hammers the ego and dissolves all the concepts and detachments. There's a beautiful story about Shri Bhausaheb Maharaj which describes how during the cremation, all that one could hear was the *Naam Mantra* emerging from his bones. This is the aim of our practice. This is the aim of the *Naam Mantra* practice. We want to remove everything that is not part of our true nature and just be that!

Allow the Spontaneous Presence to lead you

Q. Guru, you say that we must let go of the ego, the mind and the intellect. How will I cope with my work and family life without them?

A. Here you are under the illusion of being the doer, as if the person's ego, mind and intellect are doing everything, coping with everything. We know that the mind, ego and intellect are illusory. Behind these, lies the Presence. It is that Presence that makes these work. We cannot do anything without the power of the Presence.

When the ego, mind and intellect have weakened and are much quieter than before, Spontaneous Presence will come to the fore. And then, everything that was done before, will be done in the same way, but much better and more efficiently because it will be effortless. There will be no doer there. As long as we think we are doers, we are using up a lot of energy. When we know we are not the doers, we allow the Spontaneous Presence to lead us and attend to everything in life. When this happens, our daily life will be much easier and flowing.

Q. I love the Mantra and find it is very comforting, especially during concentrated meditation.

A. Again, these are concepts! Who finds it comforting or loves the Mantra? The Mantra is the sound of the breath, very natural. When people receive the Mantra a lot of them will say, "Oh this is beautiful! It's a kind of ebb and flow". Selfless Self is what we are. When you say you find it comforting, don't lose sight of the fact that there is only Selfless Self. There is no one else, nothing else within that is reciting the Mantra. There is Selfless Self alone. Therefore, Selfless Self is responding to Selfless Self. It's like the perfect rhythm, the perfect vibration, the Presence or whatever you want to call it. So, we don't have to ask questions about it. It is like we're at home with the Mantra and it's continuous and eternal, prior to beingness, after beingness. It ever exists. It goes on forever.

Only an authorized Teacher/Master should initiate

Q. The Mantra should be given by a realized Master because only he can show you your true nature?

A. No one should be giving the Mantra if they have not been authorized to give it. I already know of a few who are doing that. But if you've not been authorized to give the Mantra, or you're not a Master, then it should not be happening. Those who are giving the Mantra without authorization means that it will have no value and it's not going to work.

Q. I want to increase the repetition of the *Naam Mantra japa*. Is it okay that I hammer myself with *"I am Brahman, Brahman I am"* I relentlessly?

A. It is more than ok to hammer yourself. It is absolutely necessary! We are only able to operate because of *Brahman* because that is what we are. We identified with the mind, body, intellect and believed ourselves to be that, therefore, to establish conviction in *"I am Brahman"* instead, we need to hammer ourselves constantly with this truth. The more, the better, all the time, that will enable the shift! As Maharaj says, we need to use the thorn of truth, to remove the primary thorn of illusion, then we can throw both thorns away!

Q. I was shocked when I came across someone who had revealed the secret *Naam Mantra*. I thought it was a secret mantra.

A. Yes, we are aware of this! It is supposed to be kept a secret. That is what we promise the Master who initiates us. Maharaj's wife and son have contacted this devotee and told him to remove this video, but the person who uploaded it has refused, sadly, so there is nothing further we can do. This action has come from the ego, from someone who is power hungry and in search of gathering followers. That is all I'm going to say on the matter.

The *Naam Mantra* is not to be taken lightly

Q. I would like to be initiated with the *Nam Mantra* from the Guru.

A. What is it that you are hoping to receive from Initiation? In what way do you see that it is going to help you?

Q. Honestly, I hadn't thought about initiation in terms of: I expect this or that from it. But as I reflect on this matter now, I can say that there is in me a longing for disidentification with the body mind and for the return of the light. At the same time, I could also say that I don't expect anything from it and yet I await it with joy. I hope I am explaining myself well and not adding concern.

A. The *Naam Mantra* is not to be taken lightly. You sound a little vague about Initiation which indicates that you're not ready yet. The *Naam Mantra* is not a magic wand but a meditation tool that will help you to disidentify from the body mind. However, in order for it to work, you must appreciate and value it by longing for it and expecting something from it, instead of as you say, not expecting anything. Please contemplate more on your wish to be initiated and then get back to me. As I said, the *Naam Mantra* is not to be taken lightly, nor is it given lightly.

Q. I practiced TM regularly for six years, however, starting in 2017, there was a crisis in my path. I began to doubt whether TM was the right practice for me. I really disliked that the organization was asking so much money for its teachings. I began to doubt Maharishi Mahesh Yogi as a teacher I could follow. So, I started looking around for other teachings but didn't feel comfortable with any. I started to think more and more that maybe I should look for a new teacher and other practices. And so today, I came across Shri Ramakant Maharaj's website and I like that he also offers a Mantra-based technique. May I ask for information on how I can start practicing this Mantra?

A. Are you male or female? How old are you? Where do you live? You say you have been looking for some spiritual teachings and practice to follow for a long time. Can I ask you what you're hoping to find from them? The *Naam Mantra* is not like TM. It is not a standalone Mantra but part of the teachings and the practice. Which spiritual books have you read? You need some kind of reading background, so I suggest you start with *Selfless Self* and get back to me after you have read it.

How long should I use the *Naam* for?

Q. How long should I be using the *Naam Mantra* for?

A. For as long as it takes to purify and remove all the layers of illusion, the concepts, attachments, etc. You should use it until you are established in, and as, your true nature, without any vacillations.

First make friends with silence

Q. I would like to be initiated before I attend a retreat.

A. It's not a good idea to be initiated before that because if you attend a retreat, you should be fully present there, following the itinerary along with the others. Secondly, from the questions you're asking, I don't feel you have fully understood the teachings in *Selfless Self*. It would be better to gain more clarity and absorb them before Initiation.

You said the retreat would offer you a taste of silence, so let that be the first step. You also commented on whether you would be able to stick to the practice and that is why I think you should take one step at a time. Initiation demands your commitment. Are you ready? Attend to the retreat! Make friends with the silence and then afterwards we can meet again.

The opportunity to dive deep into the ocean of Self

Q. It has been a little over 2 months since the *Naam* Initiation, but it seems like I have been with the lineage for eons. Lots going on my end! I spent a wonderful week touring the landscape of the Self. I dedicated the entire time to the *Naam* practice.

A. I'm so pleased to hear about your recent intense practice. What dedication! You have taken to the *Naam* practice like a duck to water. It is a wonderful journey you are on and I can tell you are thriving on it, like you have been waiting a lifetime for this opportunity to dive deep into the ocean of the Self.

Q. Sometimes the Mantra seems to reverberate inside, not the same words but as a rhythmic vibration. Is it Selfless Self, or is it Selfless Self making the vibration and therefore, a sign of grace?

A. Namaste! The Mantra is vibrating, internalising. That's a good sign. It is everything you say.

You are never your experiences

Q. Three weeks ago, my head began to hurt very badly with the constant repetition of the Mantra. (The point in the centre of the head behind the eyes feels strongly compressed and the third eye seems to be on fire). This pain radiates to the veins, the back of the head, and I noticed that because of this, the jaw is strongly compressed at night. I wake up several times at night and it is difficult to fall asleep because of the pulsation in the centre of the head of the *Ajna* chakra. Also, during the day, there was a feeling of a slight loss in consciousness or as if you are going under water, even sometimes forgetting some simple things. I have not repeated the Mantra for 10-12 days, but all these effects have not gone away. Even ordinary breathing provokes the third eye to these reactions. Please let me know if there are any recommendations.

A. There seems to be an imbalance, an overloading of the mental processes. Distance yourself from what's going on. It is important NOT TO GIVE ATTENTION TO THIS PHENOMENA. As you know, if you give attention to something, it feeds and energizes it more. You are never your experiences. You are always the witness of them. So, here, you are the WITNESS of these sensations and experiences. You need to bring your attention back to centre, back to Selfless Self, back to the Heart. Everything is transient and therefore will pass. This period will also pass. The cleansing process works in its own way and at a pace that we frequently can't make sense of, but we need to trust the process anyway. You know that the *Naam* only works for "good" and cannot "hurt".

Don't let the "mind" comment so much on what is going on and don't buy into any feelings of distress or fear. Remind yourself that you are formless, prior to beingness and therefore, nothing is actually happening because you are unborn. Bring your focus back to Reality, your natural, Stateless State. When we experience what you describe as moments of partial loss of consciousness and feelings of going underwater, it is time to do Self-Enquiry. Just ask yourself, "Who is having this feeling? Who is drowning?" or "Was this happening prior to beingness?" These questions will disarm the sometimes intense, yet illusory moments that arise. If we are caught off-guard, we will "fall into the ditch" as Maharaj says - or take it for real! A reminder of the importance of staying alert at all times, so that we do not fall into any traps.

The *Naam Mantra* is not to be viewed as something isolated and separate from our Master, Shri Ramakant Maharaj. To bring back some equilibrium at this time, I recommend more devotion, *puja* to Maharaj/Sadguru. Call on Maharaj, be with Maharaj and surrender everything that currently appears to be going on, to Maharaj. Again, this will help you shift the focus of attention from the effects - the temporary, to the permanent - the Ultimate.

Finally, see this as another opportunity, challenge or test for you to be courageous and deepen your Conviction by remaining as the witness. In the face of unsettling, continuous symptoms, at the same time, you know deep down, that no matter what appearances arise, they cannot touch your Essence, your Reality that has always remained pristine, unblemished, untouched, and will always remain untouched for eternity.

Don't worry! Be assured that what is going on is an illusory, passing show. You are a Master, so, it is up to you to release the hold this phenomenon has over you and shift the focus. Stay with Selfless Self! Stay with Maharaj's shield of protection. Spend time in prayer and devotion, offering gratitude to Maharaj for the Truth He has shown you. Express your humility by bowing to Maharaj, as well as singing to Him!

You are not the doer, therefore, who is guilty?

Q. Recently a lot of reminiscing has been coming up during meditation, especially guilt regarding my past actions. I see how my egotism has hurt others in ways that I didn't before. I think you mentioned this phenomenon in one of your online videos; it's perhaps an aspect of the "purification" and I should be careful lest I identify with the guilt, as that implies doership, etc. Nevertheless, I reached out to one of the persons I arrogantly hurt many years agio, and I thought maybe she would think I had gone mad to suddenly come and apologize after all this time. Instead, not at all, she truly appreciated it and showed me a poem she had written back then and had it on the wall near the bed - perhaps that contributed to heal an old wound.

But I have to be careful not to get caught up in this personal stuff. Could it be that the more one dis-identifies with the ego, the more the ego is seen for what it is, and it ain't pretty? So naturally some guilt and disappointment arise, as in "Am I really this? Did I really act so arrogantly and selfishly without noticing?" It's also clear one has to go back to Self-enquiry as I am not the body. That is what you tell me, so my true self is also sinless. This is also something I read Ramakant Maharaj say.

When it comes to the Initiation, the thought that comes up is whether I'm worthy of it but then the answer should be to make it so, and to prepare the altar (pictures arrived), to make a welcoming environment for the Masters, and so on. Also, I read a statement from Ramana Maharshi the other day that makes mc confident I should do this sooner:

"Think of God; attachments will gradually drop away. If you wait till all desires disappear before starting your devotion and prayer, you will have to wait for a very long time indeed."

This makes me realize that if I wait until I'm perfectly pure then I'll probably have to wait "till death do us part" (me & my body, that is) ...

A. The purification process brings all the dirt to the surface. Cleansing is needed...ie., erasing all that is not true. All the layers of conditioning, experiences, identification with the body-mind complex. The purpose is to clean the slate and not to indulge in past behaviour. And guilt is a concept. Who is guilty? Were you guilty prior to beingness?

Your true nature is immaculate, unsoiled, untouched, immutable and definitely sinless. So, don't get caught up in past behaviours. You do not exist, therefore, who is the "sinner"? Who is "guilty"? You have been playing different roles in this dream life.

Don't waste time and energy making amends and apologizing. If you wish, you can make these gestures when you are more detached from the body-mind. Now the real business that awaits your energy is simply to allow everything to arise, without analyzing anything, without getting involved in the illusion of what you think you did etc. You did not do anything. No doer! The ego behaved in certain, learned ways. However, soon you will know that this all came from conditioning. As I said in a previous mail, when the ego-mind senses its impending destruction, it will fight tooth and nail for survival.

Don't get caught up in all this stuff from the past. It's not the direction we want you to go in! Self-enquiry is important to stop this train of identification!

Who is worthy? There is no such question to consider! Agreed! The sooner the better so that you can get rid of the false "I" and undergo the process of deprogramming to remove all illusion, the darkness of ignorance. Only by doing so, will the light of truth begin to shine.

When I said to you to prepare for Initiation, I did not mean you were to undergo self-analysis, I just meant opening your heart, growing in trust and sincerity and preparing your altar at home!! Now is the time for devotion, prayer and surrender. If you wait for all desires to disappear without meditation, you will wait forever. The *Naam Mantra* will assist in dissolving these and help you discriminate between the real and the unreal!

I advise making arrangements soonish, to travel for Initiation, followed by some time off work to really delve deep and continue the practice. Jai Guru!

Your doubts will delay Conviction

Q. I realize the importance of sticking to the prescribed path. Things will go on irrespective of the mind but the mind needs to be totally brought in control by the lineage path. But what happens if the Mantra becomes second nature but one is not able to get Spontaneous Conviction?

A. Remove your doubts! The *Naam Mantra* will become first nature and then there will be Spontaneous

Conviction. Have faith that this will happen, instead of entertaining the mind's doubts because these doubts will stop the Conviction from happening!

Let me be your eyes when you cannot see

Q. I have been going through a very difficult time and as a consequence, not managing to do the minimum daily practice. I was afraid of contacting you because of this.

A. Who is afraid? As you know, the *Naam Mantra* can bring up a lot of things that are not always pleasant. When this happens, don't struggle alone. Reach out to me! That is why I am here. Otherwise, before you know it, you will dig a big hole for yourself only to find yourself in a dark pit, unable to see what the problem is, never mind the solution. The Guru removes the darkness and shines a light. Let me be your eyes when you cannot see!

Feeling of emptiness and depression

Q. I feel that after reciting the *Naam Mantra* faithfully, a lot of the illusory layers have now been removed. But this has left me with a feeling of emptiness and depression. I was not expecting that.

A. Realize that you are still just in the middle of the process. You are not at the end. It is important for you to sing or listen to some *bhajans* while demolishing the pseudo self. The *bhajans* will lift your mood and distract you from these feelings of loss. These feelings are temporary and a reaction to your detachment from illusion. They will pass.

Q. Thanks for the Mantra. Now I want to be alone to journey with Maharaj.

A. It is not a good idea. You have just received the *Naam Mantra* which will begin to work and bring many issues to the surface. This is not the time to fly solo. Don't be deluded! You will not be journeying with Maharaj, but will instead be journeying with your ego!

Maya has trapped you again

Q. There were lots of different feelings arising during the last month or so and I could not make sense of anything. I felt as if my problems were growing by the day, getting bigger and bigger and I was stuck. After we spoke, I realized I should have reached out sooner.

A. That is why I always advise the newly initiated to keep in touch, otherwise, when you are alone, you might feel you are going through a mini nightmare. And yet, all you need at this time is to hear that you have been trapped by *Maya* again. The more entangled we get, the more we take it for real and so it intensifies. As you saw for yourself, just hearing that nothing was in fact happening, burst your big balloon of imaginary concepts, instantly. Now that you have had this experience, when it occurs again, please contact me sooner. This way you will save yourself much grief!

You must remove all the weeds

Q. Can I know Reality, my true nature, without the *Naam Mantra?*

A. Whether you use the *Naam Mantra* or some other cleansing tool, the fact remains that you cannot know the Reality that you are without a purification process. You must remove all the weeds and demolish your old dwelling house, in order to establish solid foundations. All the illusory layers need to dissolve. If the ego is not dissolved, then knowledge will simply sit on top of the ego and not be absorbed. To state the obvious – Self-Realization cannot occur until the total annihilation of the pseudo self has occurred!

Prioritise meditation over *bhajans*

Q. After a long time of being busy, I'm reorganising my life in order to have more time to recite the Mantra, a gift I received from you. I have for you two short questions: Firstly, sometimes, the meditation takes me to Self-enquiry: "Who am I?" or "Where does this "I" come from?" Is it okay? And the second one, when there's not enough time, is it correct to give priority to the *Naam* instead of *bhajans*?

A. When you are meditating, best to stick with reciting the *Naam*. This time should be devoted to hammering the ego. Continue with Self-enquiry after your meditation. Yes, absolutely, prioritize the *Naam Mantra* over the *bhajans*, especially in the beginning, until you are more established in your practice. If you do not have the time to sing *bhajans*, then listen to one or two of your favourite ones. Doing this before you begin meditation will energize the meditation!

How to rid yourself of fear

Q. Since Initiation, my practice has brought about self-transformation. I no longer recognize my former self! I seem to live on the borderline, flipping between illusion and reality. However, I don't seem to be able to crossover because of fear. In fact, on the edge of that precipice, I am consumed by terror. I am afraid of losing myself.

A. It is great to receive news from you. You have been popping into my head quite a few times. Great to hear that you have made a lot of progress! You know that the idea of losing yourself is not true because all that you think you will lose is illusory. But still, that fear can be overpowering. At this point, more courage is needed. Courage will come from making sure that the teachings are completely absorbed, that there is total acceptance. Having strong conviction that you are That Reality is essential and must be established within you. Secondly, here the upkeep of devotion to the Masters is also very important. Communicate with them, bow to them, surrender to them. All of this will remove the last vestiges of illusion and rid you of the fear you experience.

Brahman is what we are

Q. I want to increase the repetition of the *Naam Mantra Japa*. One doubt in this regard: Till we purify ourselves, since we are operating as the mind, body, intellect, is it okay that I hammer myself with "*I am Brahman, Brahman I am?*" Is it that we are always *Brahman*, even in ignorance and that gives us license to do so?

A. It is more than ok to hammer ourselves. It is absolutely necessary! We are only able to operate because of *Brahman* because that is what we are. We identified with the mind-body-intellect and believed ourselves to be that, so, to establish Conviction in "*I am Brahman*", instead, we need to hammer ourselves constantly with this truth. The more, the better, all the time will enable the shift! As Maharaj says, we need to use the thorn of truth, to remove the primary thorn of illusion and then we can throw out both thorns.

Time to reverse the process

Q. I have diligently followed the guidelines of 2 hours of formal meditation and I try my best to recite the *Naam Mantra* outside of meditation sessions. I fall asleep and wake up with the *Naam,* but I do get very annoyed with the trips down memory lane, when the mind takes me to some emotionally charged events from the past as well as to other mundane stuff.

A. This process you're undergoing is the purification or clearing out process, where everything rises in the mind in a chaotic fashion. So, although you may find it annoying, the *Naam Mantra* is doing its job of emptying you of all illusory concepts, experiences, sense and nonsense, if you like.

After this clear out, the mind will be quieter and therefore a space will open up for your true nature to emerge. Deep insights can also take place, simultaneously, during meditation. Images, teachings, visions, etc., these rare moments will increase. But don't expect them, look for them or strongly desire them. Try and remain neutral just reciting the *Naam*.

Some find the practice in the beginning very monotonous and rather boring, however, we need this hammering. We need this repetition to absorb the truth that we are: I am *Brahman, Brahman* I am. It has taken us a lifetime to build this pseudo identity and to be conditioned and brainwashed, so now it is time to reverse the process, decondition and brainwash ourselves with truth. Be disciplined and carry on as you are doing. All is well!

Each hammering brings us closer to the Source

Q. Has anyone ever asked this question to Maharaj? Because the *Naam Mantra* of the lineage is not a proper name like Shiva, Ram, Durga or Datta for example, as for many others Saints doing *Namasmaran*? It being understood that *Naam* is *Nirguna* but can also be referred to as *Saguna* for those just starting out. Mine is just a curiosity. In the end the name comes directly from him as recognition. But then these are all concepts. Where there is concept there is duality and separation.

A. Maharaj talked about the difference between the *Naam* and other Mantras like Ram, Shiva etc., several times. The fact is the sacred *Naam* vibration is our Source, the Source and Maharaj has gone as far as to say the *Naam Mantra* is the only Mantra that will return you to your original nature. And remember the story about Bhausaheb Maharaj? When the body was cremated, all that was heard was the *Naam* arising from his bones! There are many Mantras but the sacred *Naama Mantra* works because it is That which we are and each and every hammering or recitation brings us closer to the Source, as it erases all the layers of illusion and concepts.

Erase everything that is not part of your nature

Q. The Mantra is not working. I am not experiencing any bliss and not even seeing any bright lights. Why is it not working? I had expectations that the *Naam Mantra* would bring me peace and happiness.

A. You will not experience these things until changes take place within you. The *Naam Mantra* is a tool to help you erase all the worldly, illusory layers which you have accepted! The benefits will arise after these layers have been removed, not before! First you need to go through a cleansing process! So, be strong and determined to erase everything that is not part of your true nature.

Q. How can I manage this mind? Do I follow, as Bhausaheb Maharaj says, "Never forget the name even if the world is falling apart" or should I follow more Self-investigation? Why, I wonder, who is having these thoughts? But the only thing that gives me relief is *Naam*.

A. There are many practices as you know. As long as the mind is causing you trouble, then use all the tools at your disposal: the *Naam Mantra*, Self-enquiry, absorbing the knowledge more deeply, singing *bhajans*, etc. If the *Naam Mantra* brings relief, then keep reciting it. Thoughts keep flowing. You don't have to give them your attention. Thoughtless Reality is your goal.

Q. Is it in agreement with the lineage to say that the True identity is like a changeless background/screen on which both animate and inanimate images appear and disappear, like in dreams? Or is this another concept the mind attaches to?

A. Yes, this statement is in agreement with the lineage, and yes, it is also a concept. Use it as a teaching to guide you and then drop it.

In truth, all is one

Q. I have a great love for Jesus Christ. I feel that I am betraying his trust. Do I have to abandon my faith in the church to receive the *Naam Mantra*?

A. As I said, the lineage is all inclusive. Jesus Christ is a great master. And who is betraying? What are you betraying? More Self-enquiry is needed. Here all is one truth. You are separating everything. You should not take the *Naam Mantra* unless you're absolutely sure and free of doubts. There is no obligation to take it! Here there seems to be a conflict. Self-enquiry is the way forward before the decision is made.

Disinterest, detachment, spontaneous joy

Q. Namaste! Mother, everything is going fine. For practice I increased the hours of meditation which now lasts almost all night. I think I only sleep two or three hours a night while meditating. And yet, I'm not sleepy at work in the morning. I have lost interest in TV, deleted all forms of social media, and only use my phone to call my family. Two weeks ago, my cell phone was stolen from my hands. I was surprised that I wasn't scared or bothered in the slightest by it.

I am trying to recite the Mantra following the breath 24/7, but it is difficult. I find the things that others and especially my family do banal and superficial, and increasingly, I like spending more time alone. Every now and then, I experience gaps, as if there were no thoughts or mental disturbances, and when this happens, I smile. Also, when I read some sacred text or listen to *bhajans*, I get emotional and cry for no reason. I don't know if I should increase the hours of meditation.

A. Thank you for the update. It's an A star report of the progress that has taken place! Excellent! The demolition process you are undertaking is naturally and spontaneously, cleaning and clearing out everything that has no place in reality. The knowledge of your true nature is penetrating all the layers and levels of existence. You were already expressing disinterest last year, I remember, in the superficial activities of those around you! You have already dramatically extended the duration of the meditation. No need to increase it more as the body needs some sleep to recuperate.

Remember that when you are doing your normal concentrated Mantra meditation for 2 hours a day, i.e., focussed solely on reciting the *Naam,* you are to use the accompanying breath. But when you use the Mantra as *Japa* throughout the day and night, you do not need to align it with breathing!! This part of the process is pure mechanical hammering!

You can see for yourself the signs/evidence of your progress: disinterest in things you used to be interested in like TV, social media, socializing, etc. And then there is the detachment. When someone stole your cell phone, there was indifference to what had happened - no reaction of anger or feelings of loss! Your wish to be alone is another sign that you are getting closer and closer to Selfless Self. The pull towards the light of Self is behind all these changes. It is a natural, effortless impulse that is driving you forward!

When you witness gaps in mental activity and thoughts, there is a feeling of joy expressed in a smile. And you mention moments of spontaneous emotions, including crying while reading sacred text or listening to *bhajans*. These spontaneous moments arising from a deeper understanding of your Truth, your Reality, i.e. the absorption of knowledge, is the outcome of the removal of the illusory layers, all of which bring forth your true nature that is spontaneous. Tears of bliss may start flowing from the recognition that you are drawing closer to Source, returning Home at last, to your true nature. When this happens, do not try to figure out the "why" of it. Be happy with the not knowing which is what is happening! Just let these moments arise. They are part of the process that is unfolding. I'm very happy to hear of your progress. Keep going forward! Keep going deeper.

The *Naam Mantra* works without concentrating

Q. Is the meditation time a complete waste, if the body demands attention of one sort or another and/or there are periods of dreaming?

A. No! it is never a waste. This kind of Mantra meditation just requires the repetition of the *Naam Mantra*. If you are unable to concentrate or give it your full attention, it does not matter. The *Naam Mantra* is a vibration and by simply, silently repeating it over and over, it is having an effect which is being embedded within you.

The *lila* of Guru and disciple

Q. Will you be my Guru?

A. When someone asked Maharaj if he would be his Guru, Maharaj remained silent. Why? Because ultimately, everyone and everything are illusions. The Guru does not exist and neither does the disciple. Understand that life is a *lila*, or play and in that *lila*, I play the role of being your Guru and you play the role of being my disciple!

The Guru knows what the disciple needs

Q. In a previous Satsang you mentioned a devotee who did not take care or take responsibility for his ego. I sensed from you some anger/disappointment. It is the same austerity one feels when reading Bhausaheb Maharaj's *Naama Yoga*. The Guru is disappointed in his followers if they do not realize themselves. This is a question for myself, to which I do not know the answer. On the one hand, there is always the feeling that more can and should be done – more meditation, *japa*, more *seva*, more witnessing, etc. On the other hand, it seems that it is impossible to really speed up the process It has its own pace and any attempt to speed it up is illusory. So, the question is, who is disappointed with whom? Who disappoints whom? What is the responsibility as a devotee, really?

A. To say that you cannot do more to quicken the process is NOT true. Yes, the end goal will be reached, as and when, but you have the grace of the Masters pushing you forward and your energy. Here I am not talking about you allocating more time to the practice, but rather about your hunger to know thyself. That is in your hands. And this hunger is a driving force that propels the process. If you are lukewarm hungry and use "spontaneously" as a laissez-faire approach or an excuse that makes the goal less immediate, less vital, then that will slow down the outcome.

Regarding the Guru's disappointment, the Guru/Master plays many different roles. He sometimes expresses anger, approval, caring, etc., and disappointment. Who is disappointed and with whom when everything is an illusion? Within the *lila*, as the Guru guides the disciple to Self-Realization, he responds to the disciple accordingly. In your example, the Guru may express disappointment because he/she wants the disciple to "get it", to be free of illusion and suffering and to enjoy the bliss of reality. That is all! This expression is rooted in immense compassion!

The disciple's responsibility is to listen to, and follow, the Guru's guidance. Bow to his will and not to one's own! The Guru will administer the medicine needed by each disciple. He knows what the disciple needs, whereas in the early stages, the disciple only knows what he wants and therefore does not follow the Guru's guidance!

Liberation is from the person

Q. It has been invaluable for me to be with a realized person! It has left a lasting impression.

A. There is no such thing as a "realized person". Self-Realization happens when the illusory person has dissolved. Or to put it another way, liberation is from the person, not of the person! The person, pseudo self or ego-mind with all its concepts, ideas, self-image, etc, is an illusion. This person is who we think we are, the false identity! Our identity with the body-mind complex has obscured our real identity, our true identity. And that is why we need to remove all the illusory layers that are covering over our Presence. There can be no liberation until all trace, all remnants of the illusory person have disappeared.

Being in the presence of a Master or Guru speeds up the path to liberation as the Guru transmits Truth that resonates with the seeker and penetrates the illusory layers. In the Presence of the Guru, the obstacles are removed. If the seeker is receptive, then he will be inspired and grow in courage and determination, propelled on the journey to Self-Knowledge. In the Presence of a Master, in that timeless illumined space, energy and grace emanate and touch the seeker. The rub-off effect is everlasting.

Call of the Divine

Q. It has only been a couple of months since *Naam* Initiation but it seems like I have been with the lineage for eons. A lifetime of seeking, coupled with recent health challenges and *Naam* Initiation resulted in what can be characterized as the "perfect storm". I feel disinterested and disengaged from work and daily living. I have minimal attraction towards life's pleasures. The thought of retiring early is attractive, but I feel guilty about it. In positive terms, I cannot resist to answer the call of the divine any longer.

A. The lack of interest in worldly things is very common. Just Self-enquire about the guilty feeling. Who is feeling guilty? Remember that there is no "I", no separate individual in Reality, therefore, there is no one there to feel anything!

Here, what you are acknowledging is the truth about where you are at, as well as the strong pull that is drawing you deeper and deeper, so that you can know your true nature. Forget about the concept of guilt! What is really happening is what you clearly state in your own words: that you cannot resist the call of the divine any longer! And that is a wonderful space to be in!

Spiritually speaking, there is nothing to stop you from following your heart's longing for truth, wholeness and peace, for wishing to return Home to the place you never left. You must be true to yourself! If you are in the position to retire early in order to totally surrender to the journey, then there is nothing standing in your way. Don't delay. Your time is now! None of us knows how much time we have left in the body, therefore, we cannot take anything for granted. And you know more than most, how important it is to "wake up from the dream", as soon as possible. It is up to you to make it your last dream! The place you find yourself in is a beautiful one. You are ripe to finish the journey.

Q. A few years ago, I was going to contact you but I didn't. And now I know why I had to wait before seeing you and being initiated. This time I felt called. It was a divine call that brought me here. Looking back, I wasn't ripe but this time, so much has happened that I can't explain. All I know is that I've found what I was looking for.

A. You mentioned that a few years ago you had many doubts. These doubts would have prevented you from having complete faith in the teachings, the Masters and the *Naam Mantra*. Whereas now you are able to accept everything with complete faith, and most importantly, the value and importance of the *Naam Mantra*. You said that the experiences I wrote about with the Master in *Timeless Years* book, you are now going through similar ones. Wonderful! Keep digging deeper. Stay in touch!

Always rooted in love

Q. The last time we spoke, I felt that you were provoking me for no reason. It is not something you have done before?

A. Remember that everything is a *lila*. Sometimes when the disciple appears self-assured and maybe too pleased with himself, the Guru may test him. If you had remained silent, you would have passed the test. But instead, you defended yourself and fell back into duality, believing in an illusory "I" who was unjustifiably provoked by his Guru which, in turn, reignited feelings of anger. Remember that the way the Guru treats the disciple is always rooted in love, for the good and growth of the disciple.

The Guru's Birthday

Q. Why do you celebrate a Guru's birthday when he has transcended the body and is Self-Realized?

A. This question comes up a lot. We celebrate it because without the vehicle of the body, there can be no Self-Realization, no Gurus. Additionally, celebrating the birthday offers devotees another opportunity to express their devotion and gratitude. As the birthday approaches, the energy within and around the disciples grows in intensity and the Presence of the Master is deeply felt. Today is the unborn birthday of Shri Ramakant Maharaj. Throughout the world, devotees' hearts are overflowing with love for their Master. A special day of grace and blessings will mark this auspicious day!

Q. What kind of relationship develops between the Guru and his disciple?

A. The relationship between the Guru and his disciple is like a beautiful sacred dance filled with love and devotion. The love is pure because the Guru expects nothing. He is only interested in helping the seeker uncover his true nature.

Nisargadatta Maharaj said again and again, "I am not making you disciples, I am making you Masters". Many Gurus or teachers are searching for followers to emulate and make them – consciously or unconsciously, dependent on them. They do not empower seekers to realize their inner Master, and/or enable them to stand on their own feet. This is what Shri Ramakant Maharaj did for his disciples. He never put himself above anyone!

He always reminded them, that like every other thing that does not exist, neither does the Guru and the disciple. After all, there are no exceptions to the rule: Nothingness is always the baseline! Where was the Guru? Where was the disciple, prior to beingness? The Guru is the mirror in which you can see yourself. The Guru is a catalyst and transmitter, bringing you into the space where there is nothing, the space in which the authentic Guru abides, the Stateless State. But it takes two to tango and the Guru never imposes or coerces anyone. He cannot force a disciple to do anything.

The process of removing the layers of illusion under the guidance of the Guru, along with devotion to the Guru, bring about the merging of the illusory two! Bowing, serving, surrendering to the Guru, all help to dispel the notion of separateness, thus enabling the yoga or union with the Guru. This, in turn, leads to union with, and the realization of, your true nature.

The Lineage teaches the importance of devotion after Self-Realization because while there is no individual

Guru and no individual disciple, the process from illusion to reality is made possible by the Guru. The mystical, yet pragmatic association or dynamics between the Guru and the disciple is the catalyst. And without that, enlightenment may take many more years, or possibly lifetimes! Devotion to the Guru continues after the Guru has left the body. That said, this devotion is ultimately to Selfless Self, that one Essence that we all share!

Don't change Masters!

Q. Since Shri Ramakant Maharaj left the body, I have been tempted to go and see another Master. Is this acceptable?

A. Shri Ramakant Maharaj devoted his life to his devotees. His last message was "Don't change Masters! Your Master is like a mother and you don't change your mother!" He said this because he knew that devotees would be tempted to go elsewhere, after he had left the body.

Maharaj gave you everything. You will not find anything new or anything more, by going to see another Master. Keep the practice going and keep absorbing the teachings. Remain one-pointed! That means remain devoted to Maharaj. If you scatter yourself, divide yourself between two Masters, this will dilute your earlier commitment to Maharaj. Remember that when Maharaj initiated you, it established trust, a link or bond between the two. That bond is eternal. Maharaj has not gone anywhere. He was never the form. He is with you always. Don't fall into the trap of going to see someone new. Ask Maharaj for guidance and you will get it. You are undergoing a process of removing all the illusory layers. Stick with it. Be patient and have complete faith in yourself and Maharaj.

Q. Why is Guru Purnima so important?

A. It is a special day for honouring the Gurus who selflessly guide seekers and light the path to Self-Realization. On this day, we give thanks to the Gurus for inspiring devotees to aspire to the highest goal. On this auspicious day, we receive divine blessings that help us renew our determination.

Q. How should I behave with my Guru?

A. Always with respect. The Guru is here to guide you. You must follow his advice. Through obedience to the Guru, the seeker's ego is hammered again and again, until it crumbles.

Don't let the ego disagree with the Guru

Q. But what if I disagree with what the Guru says? What if I really know that I am right?

A. In the beginning of the demolition process, the Guru and the seeker should not be viewed as equals. If you disagree with the Guru, recognize that it is the ego that is treating the Guru as a body-mind. If you think you are right and the Guru is wrong, then, not only are you back in duality, but you have lost respect for the Guru.

You are here because you wish to be liberated from your small self. If something has not gone according to your plan or you may not like some words that have been exchanged, don't hold onto any feelings of anger. Don't let pride stand in your way and allow it to alienate you from the Guru. How much time are you prepared to waste? How long are you going to keep feeding the ego over an illusory disagreement? If you are waiting for the Guru to apologize over a body-based matter, it will not happen. The Guru has the first and the last word. The Guru is here to guide you. Realize what is going on. You are on a slippery slope, remaining small and stubborn. You have forgotten that you are *Brahman*! Therefore, start acting like *Brahman*!

Worship Sadguru - the one in all

Q. I love many Gurus and saints like Ramakant, Ramana, Anandamayi Ma. Is it ok to worship them all, or should I be more one pointed?

A. In the beginning, if you still have a limited, dual vision and see the Guru as the form, then it is better to focus on only one Guru. But afterwards, when you know that the Guru is not the form and there is only oneness, at that time, when all the gurus and saints become one in your eyes, you will worship the one in all as Sadguru, while knowing, at the same time, that you are the worshipper, the worship and the worshipped.

Q. I guess the only difference between you as Guru and me as disciple is that you know that you are *Brahman* as a living reality, while I know perhaps only intellectually, with an increasingly, growing non-intellectual knowledge. Am I right Annji ma? And, another query: the recitation of the Mantra seems to be, at this stage, a deterrent to remaining reposed in the self, (I mean it seems a movement from simple being), yet it may be premature to say this. And at this stage, I still need the *japa*. Can you advise?

A. Yes there's no difference between us, just that I know that I am That, whereas you do not yet know! Re: your query, that is the mind playing tricks with you again. As I have said many times, the *Naam Mantra* is a hammering tool that is needed to erase the "you" that is an illusory construct along with everything you imagine yourself to be - all concepts, desires, attachments, everything. You are still very much controlled by the mind, the ego and intellect, so if you wish a repose in simple, pure being, then to put it bluntly, it will not be pure being – at least, not at this stage!

All the Masters and saints are within you

Q. I have loved Bhagawan Ramana's teachings for years. Then I came across the book *Selfless Self* and Ramakant Maharaj and I was blown away by the teachings. After meditating for a few years with the *Naam Mantra*, suddenly, I am once more drawn back to Ramana. What is troubling me now is a feeling of guilt that is overpowering and tearing me apart. I am confused, as I now feel I have two Masters when I should only have one.

A. First thing is don't feel guilty. Drop the guilt! You are seeing the Masters as separate forms and that is what is causing the confusion. The Master is not the form. There is only one Sadguru! Having said this, both Ramana and Ramakant have taken you closer to Self-Realization. Yogi Ramsurat Kumar attributed his Self-Realization to three Masters – Ramana, Aurobindo and Ram Dass. But to take this further, ultimately, there are no Masters and no disciples. Where was Ramana or Ramakant prior to beingness? So, instead of being caught up in a dilemma between two Masters, turn your attention back to yourself and realize that there is nothing except Selfless Self. Everything is within you. All the Masters and saints are within you.

Q. Why is a Guru or a true authentic teacher necessary?

A. First of all, the Guru once had the same burning desire for truth which led to Self-fulfilment. Secondly, because he has walked the same path as you are now walking, he knows all the obstacles. Thirdly, in the Guru's Presence, Self-transformation quickens. The Guru is therefore the perfect guide.

When the Guru appears, it is not your imagination

Q. I was going through a very difficult time with family problems. I sat in front of my altar just being with the

Masters. Shortly after, I was looking out of the window up to the sky, I could see Maharaj. I could not believe it. I was laughing and crying at the same time. But then the mind commented that I was imagining it all. My question now is, did this happen? Did Maharaj appear to me or was it just my imagination?

A. This is wonderful! Be assured that it was not your imagination. Whenever, wherever or however the Guru appears, in visions, dreams etc., it is always Reality. Never doubt this fact. The Guru appears to show you that he is with you at all times. He appears because of your devotion. Often during some hard times when we feel battered by life and a little broken, grace manifests in different ways, to strengthen you. In your recent experience, you were gifted with Supreme grace – a blessing indeed!

After *Mahasamadhi*

Q. Would you say it is more difficult to remain faithful to the Master after he has attained *Mahasamadhi*?

A. Maharaj knew all too well that some devotees would be tempted to change their Masters, as soon as they left their bodies. This subject was in fact, the subject of his final talk, given to a group of devotees at his home. His words were: "Don't change Masters! Your Master is like a mother and you don't change your mother! If the devotee carries the misunderstanding that the Master is the form, then he may feel more vulnerable when the form is no longer there and consequently, go searching for another Master! However, if the devotee understands that the Master is formless and there has, in fact, been no change, he will know that the Master is still with him and therefore his faith in Him continues and deepens even more. For some devotees, after *Mahasamadhi*, the Presence of the Master is felt more strongly. They are graced with many dreams or visitations!

Sometimes backtracking has its place

Q. Do seekers sometimes abandon the practice, wander elsewhere but then return to the Lineage?

A. This happens! Sometimes seekers need to convince themselves, again and again, that they have made the right decision, so, they backtrack, return maybe even to a former tradition. But after sometime, they know for sure. Convinced that that is where they belong, they return to the practice!

Your connection deepens after *Mahasamadhi*

Q. If the work has not finished, I mean, if a disciple has not reached the destination prior to his Guru leaving the body, is it alright, acceptable for him to find another living Guru?

A. Why would you desire to be with another Guru! If you have been blessed with the grace of being in the presence of a living, authentic Guru, then the work will be finished. Your connection with your Guru is not severed at the time of his *Mahasamadhi*. On the contrary, it is ever deepening.

Connection with the Guru is beyond time and space

Q. Recently, I heard of one Guru saying that once grace has placed you in connection with a Guru in physical form, deviating from that is a problem. Why would it be a problem?

A. It is not a problem. The feeling of betrayal that can arise when contemplating moving away from one's Guru, will be an intense one for good reason. Because it is a reflection of the depth of this "eternal relationship" in oneness that has been forged!

Surrendering to a Guru is not time limited, ie., for as long as the Guru is in the body! The connection with the Guru is beyond time and space. If one is fortunate to meet a true Guru and is graced by Him, then this relationship in oneness of the Guru-disciple will take the disciple to Self-Realization - whether the Master is still in the body or not! The Guru-disciple relationship is beyond understanding. It is mystical/alchemical and eternal. If the work has not been completed while the Master was in the body, then it will continue and still reach completion after the Guru's *Mahasamadhi*!

Self-Realization is not a teaching qualification

Q. Are there Masters who live in obscurity? If so, is their state of Realization any less than the well-known and more publicly available Masters?

A. Yes there are Masters who live in obscurity, but why would their Realization be any less? Perhaps you are confusing Self-Realized beings to Self-Realized beings who teach? There may be many Self-Realized beings around that we do not know about, but very few teachers. Self-Realization is not a qualification to teach. Teaching is a skill!

Changing Gurus is cheap

Q. When one's Guru is no longer in the body, it can be hard for the devotee. It's not surprising then that some devotees go looking for another Guru. My question is, is this acceptable?

A. You should not change your Guru. The Guru is not the form. The true Guru is a Sadguru who has taken your hand and will walk with you for eternity. He has given his life to his devotees, therefore, to change Gurus is basically cheap. It is a betrayal of trust which shows that the devotee's trust in the Guru was never very strong. Without trust, there is no integrity.

100% guarantee of liberation

Q. I have been on the spiritual path all my life and I have been with other teachers, attending Satsangs, listening to them. But after reading *Selfless Self,* I realize now that this is the first time I have come across simple instructions to follow that are so clearly laid out. Maharaj not only stresses the necessity of a purification or cleansing process, but shows us how to do it by offering us a cocktail of Self-enquiry, Mantra, Meditation and *Bhajans*.

A. Yes Shri Ramakant Maharaj is the only Guru I have ever heard saying, "If you follow these instructions, I guarantee 100% that there will be liberation." Most contemporary spiritual teachers do not stress the importance of hammering the ego and dissolving the pseudo identity. They are happy to talk and talk and talk, ad infinitum. And more often than not, conveying mere intellectual knowledge. Yet without a cleansing process, the knowledge they are listening to, will not be absorbed. It will simply be piled on top of the ego and remain there. Various practices are necessary to absorb knowledge. As Maharaj states, "it is only through meditation that you will understand without words, what you previously could only understand using words". In other words, a firsthand direct understanding occurs!

Why do Gurus fall from grace?

Q. Why is it so often the case that Gurus seem pure to begin with. They start off well-intentioned, but then, they fall. And all we hear about them is scandal after scandal?

A. Oftentimes Gurus are not fully Self-Realized. They are maybe able to transmit *shaktipat or* spiritual energy, which deceives the seeker into thinking they are authentic Gurus. But that does not mean to say that they are completely liberated from their egos. And as has happened many times, if they are still carrying ego and start teaching prematurely, acquiring followers, etc., this will inflate their egos even further. And then it is only a matter of time before they are gripped by the 3 temptations of power, sex and fame.

The three temptations: power, money sex

Q. A similar question here. If Self-Realization is permanent, how can the Guru fall?

A. The Guru may not have undergone a purification or cleansing process which means that his awakening is only partial. The foundations are not solid because all the illusory layers of his life have not been removed. He may have some knowledge, but still, there remains some traits, tendencies, impressions, etc. And then what transpires often is that the Guru becomes famous and increasingly enjoys the attention. The result is that instead of serving his devotees, he becomes more and more self-serving.

Q. Should we, during meditation, negate everything that comes to awareness as it is a concept or perception, including, even the observer?

A. When you're meditating, don't involve yourself in discrimination and discernment at all while reciting the *Naam Mantra*. When you're reciting the Mantra just focus on the Mantra. If you switch your attention to observing the thoughts, then the hammering will be interrupted. Better to attend to Self-enquiry outside of meditation. When you're reciting the Mantra and various thoughts are coming up, don't give them your attention. Just ignore them and keep on reciting. So, stay focussed on reciting the *Naam*. Later on, you can look at things that have arisen during meditation. However, it's important to fix your concentration on the *Naam*.

When you are not reciting the *Naam Mantra*, try and remain as the witness or observer and don't allow yourself to be drawn into illusion. Staying as the witness is very important because it stops you getting caught up in worldly things. Becoming established as the witness takes time. Eventually, one goes beyond the witness.

Q. As I'm meditating with the *Naam Mantra*, there's a feeling that - and I could be totally wrong - so this is why I'm asking it - as I'm reciting it, it is the ego that's reciting and then the space, or whatever's there feels like I'm witnessing it. Is that the right way to see it during the Mantra meditation period?

A. There is no right way to see anything. When you're chanting the Mantra, what Maharaj encourages you to do is just recite the Mantra. The question about who is reciting is irrelevant. It doesn't matter who is reciting the Mantra. In the beginning, what is most important is basic hammering. The Mantra is a vibration that works by itself, therefore, whether you focus on it or not, the main thing is to get it into your system. Just recite, recite, recite. After a period of time, you can relax with it and loosen the force and focus more on its meaning. But right now, you want to get that vibration deep within you, establish it deep within you. So, forget about who's doing it, what's happening, is it happening? Keep it simple and recite!

Glimpses of the Absolute in images

Q. Is it possible that I recognize glimpses of the Absolute in Ramakant Maharaj's pictures and should we meditate, concentrate on them?

A. That's a very good question because many of you have probably seen some pictures of Maharaj where he is completely absent from the body. And you look at Maharaj's picture and you see the transcendence. He has transcended the body-mind, transcended everything. And in these pictures, you can feel a transmission from the Master, Sadguru. Yes! I would recommend that as well. I have my favourite pictures of Maharaj and they transmit tremendous power. If you focus on certain images, the energy emanates Oneness. You will feel at one with Maharaj which is what we are. There is only Maharaj! And this kind of focus on the Master's image can aid your concentration and assist you during difficult times. Oneness is there in these pictures. Definitely recommended!

The veil

Q. If we are already realized, how can illusion remove the illusion of being a body now, when we are already realized but don't know that we are?

A. There's a veil covering over our Reality and that's why we use the *Naam* to chip at the ego, the intellect and the mind. We use it to remove the layers, the concepts, the attachments, so that the realized state that we are, will come to the fore. At the moment, it is hidden under darkness. There's a lot of clutter on top. When we do the practice and remove all the layers, then the light comes to the fore and shines, until everything has dissolved.

Emulate the Masters

Q. Can we ever reach such a great level of devotion, living as we do, surrounded by people who live completely absorbed by the senses?

A. Of course, we can! The Masters did so! That is what's special and unique about this lineage, that it is a householder lineage where many of the Masters were married with families. They worked, too, and they didn't get sidetracked by the world or by work, responsibilities or by other people who weren't following a spiritual path.

They viewed the difficulties in the world as challenges for them to overcome, as well as to deepen their spirituality. They didn't have a problem juggling their home and working life with meditation. They knew that what was around them was illusion, devoted themselves to the practice and succeeded in Self-Realization. So, of course we can reach a great level of devotion. Remember that devotion is internal. If you give yourself time, allocated practice time to devote to the Masters, then it will happen. Of course it's possible! Have no doubt!

Sincerity and longing are what counts

Q. Why did Shri Maharaj keep telling those who did not have the Guru Mantra to recite "*I am Brahman, Brahman I*".

A. If seekers were not able to receive the *Naam* because they could not travel to receive it from Maharaj directly, due to illness or whatever, then Maharaj would say, use "*I am Brahman, Brahman I am*". It has the same meaning as the *Naam* and it works. Don't think in this way... that if you get the *Naam Mantra* it is a superior Mantra and you will realize, but the one who has just got "*I am Brahman Brahman I am*" will not. It doesn't work like that.

You can have the *Naam Mantra* - and I know of many people who received it but failed to value it. They do not do their practice and therefore, nothing is happening. If you use the Mantra "*I am Brahman*" and you are dedicated and completely determined to follow the path and do your practice, that earnestness, that dedication, that devotion, will take you all the way. So, whether you have "*I am Brahman*" or the *Naam Mantra*, it doesn't matter because what counts is what is in your heart, and what drives you forward is your sincerity and longing to Self-Realize.

Q. Shri Siddharmeshwar Maharaj after Realization used to enter spontaneous *samadhi* at the most unexpected moments. Did the same thing happen to great achievers like Ramana Maharshi or Ramakrishna? Because you never hear about it... and Nisargadatta?

A. Yes of course! But who wants to know? Concentrate on your practice. Concentrate on yourself and find out who you are! Forget about everything else.

Contemplation follows meditation

Q. Shankaracharya said that meditation does not lead to realization but only contemplation done 24 hours a day can show your nature. What is the difference between contemplation and meditation?

A. Meditation is about concentration or focussing on for example, the *Naam Mantra*. Contemplation is the next stage. It means churning the reality that you are, being still and dwelling, in and as, your true nature.

Q. Seeing the blue pearl/sesame seed and hearing the *Anahata Nada*, are they also to be let go of, being as they are related to the body and not known of prior to beingness?

A. Yes! Everything has to be surrendered - all the knowledge. The pointers and knowledge take us from A to B, however, once they have served their purpose, we no longer need them!

Q. I have been reading in *Selfless Self* that the Mantra "*I am Brahman, Brahman I am*" is the *Naam Mantra*.

A. You can use this Mantra until you receive the *Naam Mantra*, if you wish it. But this is not the *Naam Mantra* which is a secret Mantra that is given in private. However, its meaning is the same as "*I am Brahman, Brahman I am*". The *Naam Mantra* has a lot of power. It remains a secret Mantra in order to preserve its power. If, for example, it is exposed and becomes just like any ordinary term or words in common usage, it will lose its power.

Miracles

Q. I am excited to share that things have been happening – miracles! I was working in the office and then my attention was drawn to a map on the wall. Suddenly, the image of Shri Nisargadatta appeared on the map. I was stunned! I stared at it for a few seconds, then it disappeared. A few weeks later, I passed by a picture of my husband that was sitting on a table and then, suddenly, my husband's face changed into the face of Shri Bhausaheb Maharaj. He is the head of our lineage, a giant! I was overwhelmed. What does this mean? I am overjoyed.

A. This is wonderful to hear. I know how close you are to Shri Nisargadatta Maharaj. When the Masters appear in this way, they are encouraging you in your practice, telling you that what you're doing is correct. You're on the right track. And seeing Bhausaheb Maharaj is amazing, too. He has such authority. He is making an appearance to encourage you, bless you and reassure you that progress is being made.

These are indeed miracles. Hold onto them! Don't forget them too easily because the Masters are blessing you and gracing you with their Presence. Many seekers long for these kinds of experiences. Don't take them lightly! When such things happen, make sure you express your deep thanks to them. Be humble and bow to them. When times are difficult, remember these moments. They will give you strength and courage to overcome the problems.

Q. After the *Naam Mantra* and still within meditation, there arose faces of anonymous individuals appearing and then disappearing within space. This was followed later, by a very high-definition view of a busy populated street scene within that space.

A. It is an example of how everything is projected from your inner Presence.

Keep in touch

Q. Do you have any additional advice for this journey?

A. I have plenty of advice but first I would like to know what is going on with your practice. Any experiences, insights, changes? Have you noticed changes in your daily life? It has only been a few months since your

Initiation. Throughout this time, you have kept up the practice with discipline, so, keep going and stay in touch. I know you have said a few times that you want to be left alone, but this is not advisable in the beginning. I have been on the journey and therefore can guide you and let you know how to avoid the pitfalls. When you are engaged in the process, it is not easy to see clearly for yourself what is going on, therefore, please keep in touch.

The divine plan has come to fruition

Q. I attended the retreat for just four days, instead of ten. I had some strange experiences, some deep meditations, but overall, it was not what I needed. The teachings were so watered down and full of platitudes compared to the Ultimate Truth. So, I decided to leave early. Now that I have some free time, I would love to visit you, if there is a way and you are available.

A. Yes of course! Come! All along, I felt you should come for Initiation instead of going on this Retreat. Now the divine plan has come to fruition.

Do you still identify as a Buddhist?

Q. I have been a practicing Buddhist for over 40 years, Now I am reading and listening to Shri Ramakant Maharaj, hammering to me that I am the Spontaneous Presence and the world is a projection. Well, this is all deeply resonating with me! I have been using *"I am Brahman, Brahman I am"*. Is this the Mantra? If not, is it possible for me to hear it? I have no other interest in life except returning to the home I never left.

A. Can you tell me how old you are? The Mantra has the same meaning as "*I am Brahman, Brahman I Am*", but it is given by way of Initiation which Shri Ramakant Maharaj authorized me to do. Please tell me which books of Maharaj you have read? Do you still see your identity as a Buddhist? I am not sure if you understand that the *Naam Mantra* is not simply a separate stand-alone Mantra but something that is an integral component of the lineage teachings? Are you familiar with the Masters of the Inchegiri Sampradaya? If not, please take a look at the website.

Q. I went through the website and learned about Maharaj. Let me give you my brief background: I live in Pune, India and have worked in Bombay, too. My age is around 40 and my spiritual journey started around 2011. I belonged to a spiritual family but I was a non-believer till 2011, when one Thursday, I had a mysterious vision of Shirdi Sai Baba. Subsequently, I started having many mystical or yoga experiences, though I hadn't practiced anything in this life. This sparked my thirst.

In the subsequent ten years, I studied many spiritual books such as *Autobiography of a Yogi* by Shri Paramahansa Yogananda, books by Ramakrishna and many other saints. I am mostly of a devotional mindset but I do practice meditation. In 2017 I read *I am That* a little but it was difficult for me to understand it, initially. I kept reading in between and I don't know, but some words stuck deep inside and something changed. So, I also read *Seeds of Consciousness*. The words were strong enough to put me into deep silence and at the same time, I had a vision of Maharaj in a dream. I have also visited the *samadhi* of Maharaj in Mumbai.

After searching for his living disciples, I found the name of Shri Ramakant Maharaj. I wish I could have met him in Nashik, but he passed away in 2018. I was wondering if I could come across anyone presently in the lineage of the Navnath Sampradaya to learn more about it.

A. Thank you for sharing your information. I am part of the lineage and was initiated in 2013. I have been initiating sincere seekers since 2018. And as I mentioned, I am the editor of Maharaj's books and I've also written two in the last couple of years: *Timeless Years with Shri Ramakant Maharaj* and *Who am I?* Let's arrange a date to meet up online.

I am crying while writing to you

Q. I cannot express in words to you what it means to me to have an opportunity to meet with you and hopefully in this lifetime have the Initiation Ceremony with you. I am crying while I'm writing this. Therefore, I'm asking if I may please come to you in person?

A. I can see how important this is for you, but let's take it slowly and first of all meet online. As I suggested, first of all, we need to explore where you are at and if you can commit to the requirements. I need to make sure that

Initiation is right for you, at this time. Maharaj hammered into me more than once, to use discrimination when giving the *Naam Mantra*. I always do so.

Bhajans – too Indian?

Q. Westerners have a tremendous block regarding singing the *bhajans*, saying they are too Indian! And in Nisargadatta's day, he did not demand Westerners to sing them. He only shared knowledge.

A. This controversy over the *bhajans* has been going on for decades. But what you say is not entirely true. Some westerners like Jean Dunn and others, did attend the *bhajan* sessions. And when they did, Nisargadatta was pleased to see them there. These seekers knew that their journeys required more than just listening to the knowledge conveyed by Nisargadatta.

Nisargadatta's editors avoided mentioning devotion

Q. If we are supposed to be singing *bhajans* as part of our practice, then why is there so little mention of them in the Nisargadatta books?

A. That is not entirely true. His early editors in the 1970's probably did not wish to put off Western readers, by including the *bhajan* practice, so, they focused pretty much entirely on the knowledge. And it was not just that they omitted references to the *bhajans*, they really avoided mentioning anything to do with devotion. Again, probably because they knew this would alienate western readers as well!

Programme days to honour the Masters

Q. I just found the online recordings of various gatherings in honour of the Lineage Masters. I did not know you did these, that they were happening. I watched the one in honour of Shri Ramakant Maharaj before going to bed. It was beautiful! The group's singing came straight from the heart, very devotional. And parts of it replayed all through the night. Beautiful!

A. We strive to mark the important dates on the Indian calendar, to celebrate the anniversaries of the Masters' "births" and "deaths". These days are very special because we have a great opportunity to express our gratitude to the Masters. As we sing to them and read passages from their teachings, we receive further encouragement to deepen our practices. Meditation on these days can be very special, too, due to the collective energy directed towards the Masters. These days are blessed, grace-filled and beautiful, giving us the opportunity to increase our humility, love and devotion.

Focus on the task at hand

Q. I am looking forward to meditation every day. For the first time in a long while, I get deep into it and I don't want to come out. I am seeing the dark blue indigo curtain after a few minutes. The spiritual eye is usually depicted with a star in the centre. Too much importance is placed upon it I think, but it's nice to look at that strange little speck of light in a deep blue sea.

A. It is great to hear that you are no longer having to push yourself to meditate. Something has changed! Seeing the dark blue curtain, as you describe it, has motivated you. However, don't give it too much importance or expect to see it each time you meditate. Don't be attached to it at this early stage in the process. Just keep hammering yourself with the *Naam Mantra*. You need to clear out everything that does not belong to you: all the layers of conditioning. Focus on the task at hand.

Too attached to the Master's form?

Q. Silly question...can you tell me if the Western devotee who was the ashram manager in Nashik is still there? He was close to Shri Ramakant Maharaj and stayed there for over 2 years, I believe.

A. A few people have been asking about him. He has not made any contact with the ashram and just seems to have disappeared. Sometimes when a devotee is close to the Master and subsequently, the Master leaves the body, the devotee feels abandoned and lost. When this happens, it means that the devotee was maybe too attached to the form of the Master. When I was at the ashram some weeks before Maharaj's *Mahasamadi* and we witnessed Maharaj's failing health, some devotees were already showing their desperation over the imminent loss. They were sobbing and agitated. Others were clinging excessively to Maharaj's feet, when they had the rare opportunity. I told one of them off at the time, saying, "Have you not learned anything? The Master is not the form. When the body expires nothing will change". But still the crying continued. Therefore, I suspect that if this particular devotee was too attached to the form, he may now be feeling a little lost.

During Maharaj's parting talk at his home, when a group of devotees were gathered around him, Maharaj, although weak, stressed, in no uncertain terms, that we were not to change him as our Master after he leaves the body. "The Master is like a mother", he said, "and you don't change your mother". Sadly, to my knowledge, some devotees have already done this.

Q. I still receive emails addressed to Maharaj from seekers who think he's still in the body form, like this one: "I, with my wife and son would like to visit the "Nashik Road Ranjit Ashram", to have Darshan of Sadguru Ramakant Maharaj to spend some time at his holy feet and receive his grace. I would greatly appreciate it, if you kindly guide me in this regard, and tell me the next availability.

A. Maharaj left the body in 2018!

Q. I was saddened to learn this that happened a long five years ago. I am now somewhat bewildered, trying to understand the significance of the spontaneous inspiration to meet Maharaj, so late now. If you please allow me to make a request to you, I would appreciate to receive some select reference links to Maharaj's pointed teachings.

A. The spontaneous inspiration to meet him means that you are to be acquainted with Maharaj's teachings. Please have a look at the website and you may be interested in reading Maharaj's various books on his teachings, namely *Selfless Self, Ultimate Truth* and *Be With You*. Let me know if I can help you in any other way!

A sweet idea but just nonsense!

Q. I would be very happy if you would initiate me. It would be good if my wife could also be initiated in the same breath.

A. Any request for the *Naam Mantra* must come directly from the one who wishes it. It is a nice idea about your wife receiving it, too, but let's just concentrate on you. I sometimes get these requests from couples who seem to do everything together and therefore, they express their wish for a joint initiation. This may be a sweet idea, but really it is just nonsense!

Bhajans are about opening your heart and surrender

Q. I'm anxious about singing the *bhajans*. How can I learn them when they are in the Marathi language? Do I need to memorize them for the initiation?

A. Don't be anxious! I'm not looking for perfect singing. Just follow the words phonetically. The singing is about opening your heart and surrendering to the Masters. You don't need to memorize the *bhajans*, as we will be singing together from the page!

Don't be a grasshopper!

Q. I'm dipping into the lineage books: some Ranjit Maharaj, some Ramakant Maharaj, etc.

A. Don't be a grasshopper! Best to stick with Ramakant Maharaj's books for now and not jump around. After all, even though the different Masters teach the same thing, each Master advances the teachings, further simplifying it for our age. Hence Maharaj's teachings are direct and tailored for our age. Plus, his teachings leave no room for the mind! There is nothing there to entertain the mind - just pure and relentless hammering.

Our journey is everyone's journey

Q. I hope this finds you well immersed in Guru's Grace. It has been exactly a month since I received the auspicious *Naam Mantra* Initiation and for that, I will be eternally grateful. I read and reread *Timeless Years* and must acknowledge yours and Charles' generosity in displaying your Love Affair between the Guru and disciple, so innocently and openly, for all to partake.

A. Thank you! Generosity does not come into it! There is no me, no Charles and no you. Our journey is everyone's Journey, the True Yoga. When there is Oneness with the Guru there is, simultaneously, Oneness with Selfless Self.

Q. What are some signposts to validate or confirm that I am making progress?

A. Fewer thoughts, a quieter mind, being less reactive, being more at peace and experiencing less stress.

Don't entertain this question!

Q. Of course, I know you will ask me to somehow get it done with Spontaneous Conviction in this very life. But did Maharaj ever discuss what would happen in the case of someone who got initiated, but the full process was not completed because the incumbent's life was cut short? Will the Masters oversee his journey in the next life also, and if so, how, just curious?

A. You should not entertain this question. The fact is you have the opportunity now in this life to Self-realize. You have all the tools at your disposal. You have the determination, so there is no reason for it not to happen. If your life is somehow cut short but you have been sincere up to that point with your practice, then the Masters grace will work on your behalf, to complete the process!

You are missing the basic teachings

Q. I have one doubt. If the Masters are still around in some way, doesn't it beg the question as to how they can have an individuality when they have merged in the Supreme? I am missing something here, but please help clarify?

A. What you are missing is the basic teachings, that do not concern only the Masters, but every one of us! We are not separate individuals. We are one Essence,

Presence. The individual, so-called, is an illusion consisting of the 5 elements. We are formless, not the form! The Masters are one Presence, just as we are one Presence. You are using the mind to try and understand what is beyond the mind!

We are all a part of that Supreme Divinity. It is our Source. We have always been that eternal Source. The forgetting of our identity is what makes us believe in the illusion that we are "somebodies" or separate "I"'s. Because we are linked to these eternal Masters, they are always with us. Nisargadatta explains this partly when he says: 'When the *Jnani's* body dies it dissolves into the five elements. If a disciple calls on the *Jnani*, his form will appear to him. His body is always present in the 5 elements, but not concentrated".

Stop creating blocks for yourself

Q. As you said, perhaps my real *sadhana* is only happening now. The question is: do I have enough time? Did the Master ever talk of this getting resumed next life, as a continuation of the process, self-driven and also blessed by the Master?

A. You asked this before! Your doubts are creating blocks for yourself. Time is a concept! With your good intention, sincere earnestness and the grace of the Master, Self-Realization will happen. Maharaj guarantees you 100 per cent, that if you follow the practices outlined, then there will be Self-Realization!

Be at peace with not knowing

Q. I imagine that the *Jnanis* must retain a little spark of ego to enable them to still be around us?

A. Re: your question, you are thinking from the perspective of the mind and trying to work it all out intellectually. There is no ego, no subtle ego. There is only *Brahman*. The *Jnanis* do not retain any ego. Impossible! Be at peace with what you cannot understand. Be at peace with not knowing. *Brahman* is all...Nisargadatta says regarding Masters and devotees: "The concept is yours; the image is mine!"

Puja - Worship

Q. How to do *puja* or worship to the Masters?

A. There is no set way of doing puja to the Masters. Be guided by your heart's devotion to the Masters and let it happen, spontaneously. If you have an altar at home with the images of the Masters, then surround them with flowers. Light a candle. Prostrate on the floor facing the Masters with an attitude of surrender. If you cannot manage to complete a full prostration, then simply bow to the Masters with a heart full of love. Light some incense. Circle the incense clockwise, in front of the Masters, concentrating on one Master at a time. Let any words arise spontaneously. Offer yourself to the Masters and ask for their guidance. Also, thank them for all that you have received from them.

Make it a regular practice to bow to each Master because He is the impersonal, unmanifest Absolute in manifest form. Each time we bow, we remove a little more ego, thus growing in humility. And through our reverence and devotion to the Master, we draw closer and closer to our inner Master.

Truth replaces falsehood

Q. One query - and to keep me motivated on the path - as one progresses on the path of *Naam Mantra* meditation and *japa*. will there be any changes along the way? Of course, the final impact is Spontaneous Conviction?

A. Yes indeed, and you have already demonstrated some of these in yourself. Basically, the things that used to bother the mind-body and have a strong hold over you - because you accepted and took them for real - will not bother you any longer. The more the *Naam Mantra* is absorbed within you, the less power these illusory attachments will have over you, till gradually, there will be nothing left. And even when these do surface now, they will touch you less, not really affect you because the knowledge is being absorbed and the truth of "*I am Brahman*" is replacing the falsehood of "I am so and so", with all its associations.

Lifelong devotion to Ramana will aid surrender

Q. As far as my problems go, I am finding that surrendering whatever transpires to *Brahman* is best.

Everything is getting impinged on the one consciousness or *Brahman*. While the *Naam Mantra* will remove the impurities that cloud my true nature as *Brahman*, surrender stemming out of a sense of helplessness will keep me sane moment by moment.

A. Yes! As I said, find what works for you. Surrender out of a sense of helplessness is powerful. You can also surrender out of pure devotion for the love of Sadguru - be that in the form of Ramana or Ramakant? You have had a lifelong devotion to Ramana, therefore, it should help the surrendering too. "Not my will, but thy will be done!"

Words cannot describe Shri Ramakant's greatness

Q. You told me that Ramakant Maharaj chose the title for the new book! My first reaction to the title *"Who am I?"* was, "How could a title the same as Bhagavan's little book be used? Another concept, I quickly realized. But it is really good for me. After reading passages from *Who am I?* it makes for a clearer understanding of *Selfless Self*! Thanks to you and Maharaj! He has truly carried on with Bhagavan's legacy – Bhagavan's "Who am I" customised for the modern age! You are his instrument to make it fructify. The Sampradaya is there and I hope there are other members doing their silent bit! May many more benefit! Shri Ramakant... incredible! Words cannot describe his greatness! Like Bhagavan, the world will slowly, but surely, know his immense contribution!

A. I say "Amen" to that! Jai Guru!

Who does not like the idea of bowing?

Q. I don't see why we should be bowing to the Masters. I don't like the idea of it.

A. Who is saying this? Who does not like the idea of it? This is ego-talk. In the Lineage, the teachings are Advaita, non-dual which includes devotion which is non-dual. There is no difference between the Masters and you. But as long as your perspective is based in duality, you will imagine a separation, a difference, two instead of one. There is only One. When we do *puja*/worship to the great Masters and bow to them, we are showing reverence to them and expressing our gratitude for all they have shared with us. At the same time, we are bowing to That one Essence, the one Reality, call it Selfless Self, that is in us all. The simple act of bowing has the effect of chipping the ego, making it less controlling in one's life. Put simply, it brings about humility.

Don't fight or love fear because it is an illusion

Q. I'll share my experiences as briefly as I can. I've been familiar with non-dualism through the teaching of Nisargadatta Maharaj for a couple of years. Since then, I've been practicing focussing on the "I am" state regularly, and it led to transformative events in my life.

The first explicable outcome was that I've naturally started to follow my intuition in all actions. It led to a massive change in the physical reality around me. My aspirations started to become fulfilled quickly. Another thing that I've noticed is the detachment from all things physical, including my body. I started to perceive the physical reality as a kind of dream. In this dream, I can follow my fears or my desires and the outcome depends on how I consciously distribute my attention. I am aware that it is my choice that anything appears in my life or not. And even though this dream is often pleasant, I can't stop thinking of waking up.

Also, even though I don't perceive myself as a body, I am aware I still have the deepest fear of dying. It keeps me from complete detachment, which I feel is something necessary to progress. To fight the fear, I often used to do something that frightened me, but it does not seem to work here. Recently, I've experienced something that I can call "loving the fear". Might it be the solution?

A. There is no birth and there is no death. You are unborn. You do not have to either fight or love fear because it is an illusion! The fear is coming from the pseudo ego, from who you think you are - ie the mind-body complex. You are not that!

In order to be liberated from the small self and its associated fears, what is needed is to absorb the knowledge of your true nature, and grow in the conviction, that you are not the body and never were. When the pseudo self dissolves, the ghost of fear will also vanish! Recognize that this life is a long dream and you are the witness, even beyond the witness. The *Naam Mantra* helps us to dissolve the ego and the illusory layers that have covered over our Presence, our Reality - that One Essence in which we all share. We are not separate beings but part of the one, omnipresent Reality.

Q. Can you give me some clarification on these 3 points please?

1. When reciting the *Naam*, do I have to remember and feel the meaning of the Mantra, or just focus on the sound/vibration of the Mantra?

2. What are some signposts to validate/confirm that I am making progress?

3. You mentioned that the cocktail Maharaj prescribes consists of reciting the *Naam*, singing *bhajans*, absorbing the knowledge and remembrance of our true nature 24/7. But one step at a time. How will I know when to take the next step?

A. 1. In the beginning, it is enough to focus on the sound/vibration. Later on, you can dwell more on the meaning.

2. Signposts would be fewer thoughts, a quieter mind, being less reactive, more peace and less stress.

3. Stay focussed on reciting the *Naam Mantra* at least for the first few months, then you can begin to integrate it with the practice of Self-Enquiry, etc.

Q. Could you clarify "apart from Selfless Self, there is no *Atman, Brahman,* etc"?

A. Many seekers think or believe that *Atman/Brahman* or Reality ... that that Reality is separate from them. When Maharaj emphasizes that there is nothing except Selfless Self, he means that you are that Selfless Self, *Atman* or *Brahman.* That nothing exists apart from the Reality that you are. Everything is within you. There is nothing else, nothing more, nothing apart from the Reality that you are.

Who is the pilgrim?

Q. Bhagavan said that Girivallam or circumambulating round Arunachala is helpful, as it has a cleansing effect. What do you say?

A. Girivallam alone is not going to awaken the seeker. He needs to know who is going on the pilgrimage around Arunachala. Maharaj used to say: "Why torture the body with this endurance test, when what is needed is guidance?

Q. The Arunachala pilgrimage and visits to other holy places, don't they help *sadhaks* at all? What is their place in the scheme of things?

A. On their own, these pilgrimages do not help. One must have spiritual knowledge that is absorbed and made one's own, in other words, pragmatic knowledge. There must be a daily practice that removes the ego and takes the seeker within, so that he knows who is going on pilgrimage. Otherwise, Girivallam remains an activity outside oneself. As if something real is out there! Nothing is outside ourselves; everything is within.

On the other hand, if a seeker is beginning to absorb spiritual knowledge and practising meditation and has strong faith in the Master – whoever he may be – then Girivallam or pilgrimage can help. The seeker can be blessed and receive the grace of the Masters. Pilgrimages are there also for the more advanced seekers, to express their gratitude for the Self-knowledge, liberation, etc. As I mentioned already, my observation while in Tiruvannamalai earlier this year, was one of many lost seekers who were literally walking around in circles. Without asking the question, "Who is the pilgrim?" means they are expecting something magical to happen to them, that is coming from outside. This is a pointless exercise!

We are not ordinary at all. There is only *Brahman*

Q. A persistent thought that creeps in is: How is it appropriate to chant "*I am Brahman, Brahman I am*" before the purity is reached because we are just ordinary beings. And how is the *Naam Mantra* synonymous or akin to other mantras in invoking the grace of *Brahman*, and yet different. Please throw some light when you get the time.

A. We are not just ordinary at all! There is only *Brahman* and the one who says we are ordinary, and only sees that, is Maya. We do not have to become pure or reach purity because we are already That. The *Naam Mantra* does not just remind us of our true identity like many other mantras, but it is a powerful tool that hammers the ego and removes the many illusory layers which have appeared, due to worldly conditioning.

Carry forward the meditative energy

Q. During meditation practice, I am able to be in reality. There are few thoughts now. But when I return to the world, so to speak, I am no longer anchored in reality. So, my question is how to remain in Reality?

A. As you know, everything is an illusion. But knowing this, theoretically, is not enough. You must really be convinced of it and accept it, in order to apply the knowledge to your daily life. Try and carry forward into the day the energy, the peacefulness and thoughtlessness experienced during meditation. The world is full of attractions and distractions which can pull you in different directions, if you are not anchored firmly in your truth, your reality. To stop this from happening, remind yourself several times daily, that everything and everyone is an illusion.

Try and stay as the witness, detached from what appears to be going on around you. Remind yourself that nothing is happening. When unhelpful thoughts arise, refuse to give them your attention. Be alert so that you can catch the thoughts before they catch you. Keep the *japa* going during difficult situations or when the body is under stress. Remind yourself that this is a dream and don't take each and every apparent challenge so seriously. Stay light-hearted, when the going gets tough. Refer to the pocket book, *Be With You* when you forget to remind yourself of reality. It is filled with strong and effective quotes from the Source that will penetrate the illusory state and bring you back home quickly. That is enough for now.

Reverse the order

Q. Every morning when I wake up, I get up and greet Sri Annji Ma, Ramakant, Lineage Masters and Selfless Self. Then I give thanks for waking up, for another blessed day, for this opportunity to get rid of the illusion and recognize true identity! I do the same thing before going to bed. On the one hand, it is useful from the point of view of showing reverence and devotion. On the other hand, it is done from the position of the body-mind, which considers itself separate. Is there more benefit or harm in such a thing?

A. It is a good thing to do! But I would reverse the order. Give thanks first to You as Selfless Self for waking up!

Conviction starts intellectually

Q. The whole practice is performed from the position of the body-mind. In fact, this is what happens: although I speak to the Masters, I actually look inside and speak to the Invisible Listener, Selfless Self. I used to worship images as separate objects, but lately, even though I bow to the images, in fact, inside myself, I worship That which projects these images.

A. Good, no separation. It does not matter. Conviction starts intellectually, until it is spontaneous. By thanking Selfless Self daily, you are repetitively hammering, the Truth that you are which has an effect.

Don't give attention to illusory problems

Q. I am trying to keep up the practice and meditate 2 hours a day. But then problems come along, people dump things on me, difficulties at work and then I feel as if I am back to square one. I don't think I'm strong enough to overcome all these.

A. Who is saying all this? Do not be a slave of your mind, listening and reacting to everything and everyone around you. You are not a slave; you are a Master. It is up to you whether you carry on listening to all the illusory thoughts and people, or instead, use discernment and separate out illusion from reality. Train yourself not to give your attention to these problems and difficulties. Use discrimination actively! Anchor yourself in Reality, in Selfless Self. You may not be able to control what comes your way, but you have total control of how you respond.

Will you let this or that illusion sting you, drag you into the ditch, or will you remain as the witness and not be touched? Accept your Reality, stay with Reality and with courage and determination refuse to leave your centre. You have the power. Convince yourself of that and stay with the Truth that you are. Keep reminding yourself when old habits and patterns appear, that there is nothing except Selfless Self and you are That!

Casual spirituality

Q. I am really grateful to you for initiating me but I cannot attend the weekly meetings and other celebrations. I still have a life at home and with work I'm under a lot of pressure. I did not realize it was going to be such a commitment!

A. Don't feel pressurized. Do what you can. You did commit to the 2 hour a day meditation, so, if that is all the time you can allocate to meditation, it's fine. However, there are many others in similar situations who are able to find the time to attend these extra gatherings. The more involved you are, the quicker you will see results. As Maharaj used to say "casual spirituality does not work".

Is it ok for spiritual teachers to charge money?

Q. Is it ever ok to pay money to a Spiritual Teacher? I know what the Lineage says about that, but I was just wondering if there might be an exception, for say, an amazing, Western spiritual teacher, one who is in demand?

A. If we are talking about authentic spiritual teachers... whether Indian or Western, the answer is No! There are no grounds for a spiritual teacher to charge money, as he is not selling you anything, or giving you anything you do not already have. All the knowledge is within you. It is innate but covered with the dust of illusion. The job of an authentic, spiritual teacher or Guru which means the "remover of darkness" – is to shine a light on you to enable you to see Reality, the one Reality which we all share.

The best day of my life

Q. This day has been the best day of my life. Being initiated with the *Naam Mantra* is such a blessing! I have meditated for years with different Mantras, but this feel different. I can feel the power!

A. You have done your preparation and are taking it very seriously. That is the only way! It is not just today, but every day! Really value what has been given to you!

Expect conflict!

Q. I am very happy and very grateful, but I am a little anxious that when I return home, whether I will be able to practice every day, from morning till night!

A. Don't allow this doubt to arise! Don't listen to it! As I have already warned you, this Mantra is a cleansing tool designed to sweep all the illusion away. It will bring up a lot of garbage, including many doubts. There will be conflict! So, you must be on guard and have courage and determination. And I am here for you!

Self-Realization must be the priority in your life

Q. In your experience, do many devotees give up before really trying?

A. There are very few! Initiation is not given lightly. Maharaj used to say, make sure that you are ready for Initiation, in other words, make sure it is right for you. If you harbour any doubts about it, then don't go forward, as these doubts will continue. You will not be giving yourself a fair chance at the outset. Secondly, Self-Realization must be the priority in your life, at the top of your list, so to speak. You will only overcome all the obstacles if there is an unceasing and profound drive to "know thyself". This drive has the power to knock down and demolish all the illusory obstacles on the way!

Grace has a part to play

Q. Are you sometimes surprised by the ones who fall away from the path and those who remain steadfast?

A. First of all, there is no path! And no, I am not surprised because beyond what we may know of a seeker before he is initiated, such as his or her spiritual maturity, there are other forces at work, as well as grace which has a part to play!

You did not come and you did not go

Q. I am amazed at the power of *Maya*. When I was with you, everything seemed so easy and I was absorbing every word you said to me. And yet on my return home, instantly, all these doubts and fears are arising. I feel weak already.

A. You are with me still. Nothing has changed. You did not come and you did not go! The body moves from A to

B. You do not! It is natural to have these moments. I warned you that after Initiation, a lot of illusory concepts, emotions and distractions would surface. Carry on with the hammering. As Maharaj says, these internal tenants do not wish to be evicted, therefore, there will be conflict. It is all part of the cleansing process. Be strong! You know that all these appearances are imaginary, therefore, don't give them attention. You are in charge. You have the power to sweep them all away. Keep in touch.

You have chosen to keep chasing rainbows

Q. I made a promise to you to value the sacred *Naam Mantra* and to keep up the practice. After a few weeks, something happened to make me realize, that I should not have taken initiation. It has nothing to do with you as a teacher, it's me. There's something wrong with me! I now feel very guilty.

A. There is nothing wrong with you! The mind is fickle. Basically, you have chosen to follow the mind and keep roaming, instead of honouring your promise. Making a promise must mean something, otherwise don't make it! And there is no point in feeling guilty! Guilt is a concept. People wallow in guilt all the time, it is just a way of disowning or not facing up to their actions which brings them some kind of absolution! You were given a golden opportunity to wake up from the dream of life and "know thyself", but you have chosen instead to keep chasing rainbows!

Surrender of the finite to the infinite

Q. I want to tell you about my breakthrough. I have always been "in my head", so to speak, consuming knowledge. When I was initiated, I told you that devotion seemed unnatural to me. I did not understand what you meant by surrender. I thought devotion was a practice in duality, etc. Well, now all this has changed! By grace, so many changes have taken place. I can't thank you enough.

A. Whether one is drawn to knowledge or devotion, surrender is essential! The small, finite, ever changing illusory superimposition one imagines oneself to be, must inevitably surrender to the infinite, unchanging, one Reality of which we are all a part.

No need of externals!

Q. I am looking for ways, techniques to speed up the process, to deepen the meditation. For example, using a *mala* while reciting the *Naam*, keeping Maharaj's ashes close to me during the practice. Is that ok?

A. It is the mind coming up with these new ideas to keep you happy and alleviate boredom! Just know that the process you are undergoing will unfold naturally and spontaneously, without externals!

Nisargadatta Maharaj singing *bhajans*

Q. I love Nisargadatta Maharaj's teachings. The knowledge is so direct. Recently, I watched a video of him doing *puja* and singing *bhajans*. The commentator said that he only did this for those who could not understand the knowledge he was sharing!

A. This is a misunderstanding! Worship and devotion go hand-in-hand with knowledge. What is the use of intellectual knowledge? Knowledge must be absorbed and applied. It must ascend from the head to the heart. Devotion after liberation is the natural continuum.

Q. I thought Nisargadatta Maharaj attained Self-Realization by himself, as if he came out of nowhere? But now I understand that he was part of a lineage of Masters!

A. This is another misunderstanding!

Sri Nisargadatta's devotion to Sri Siddharameshwar

Q. Nisargadatta Maharaj himself said many times that it was because of his Master, Shri Siddharameshwar, that liberation took place. Therefore, there is a spontaneous impulse to worship and express gratitude. Devotion to the Masters who enabled the Realization of their disciples runs through the whole Lineage of the Inchegiri Navnath Sampradaya. Nisargadatta Maharaj's devotion to Siddharameshwar Maharaj has been played down, even omitted in the literature, as it is very much an alien concept to rationally-minded Westerners!

If there is fear, there is no Conviction

Q. When I am around some people who are very ill or dying, the fear about my own mortality arises. When I do meditation, the fear subsides somewhat, but it never goes away completely. You can read about death and become tranquil, but still, when I think about it, the fear arises. I am not able to face death. Ramakant Maharaj says there is nothingness, and in the nothingness, there is the fulness. You return to the ocean of awareness. One thing I'm not clear about is whether this body, this entity, will stay?

A. At the end of the bodily life, everything dissolves. For Conviction, we need to erase the ego, quieten the mind, let the mind drop back into Source. Use the *Naam Mantra* to keep hammering yourself. As long as fear is still around, it means you don't have the Conviction that you are That, that you are beyond the body mind, that you are eternal, omnipresent - that you are the Presence behind everything. It is easy to read, but absorbing the knowledge takes more time.

Sing with a pure heart

Q. I've always had a problem with the *bhajans*. I don't have a good voice either.

A. Many people have difficulties with the *bhajans*. And it does not matter if you do not have a good voice. The *bhajans* are expressions of devotion. What is important is not your voice, but that you sing with a pure heart!

New name – new attachment!

Q. It would be nice if you gave me a name. If you did, what would it be?

A. It may be nice, but it won't help you. We are trying to get rid of all identifications, so, if I were to assign you a name, it will just become a new layer, another attachment.

Have no doubt that Maharaj spoke to you!

Q. As I bowed to the image of Maharaj during the Initiation, I heard him speak to me, saying, "Have faith. You must have faith!" Was that real? Did Maharaj actually speak to me, or was it my imagination?

A. At the beginning of the Initiation ceremony, I told you that Maharaj's Presence will be felt, and it was, strongly! Whenever and wherever the Guru appears or speaks, it is always real. Have no doubt that Maharaj spoke to you!

Self-Realization is the only religion

Q. I am afraid of losing my religion, my faith, if I follow this path?

A. Nisargadatta Maharaj said, "There is only one religion – Self-Realization". This knowledge is the highest because it is not a belief system or tradition or religion. It is about finding out who you are and knowing the Self… Self-Realization. It is direct knowledge which asks to rid yourself of all layers of identities. We are not disrespecting religion and your values but religion is man made. This path begins prior to the body form, before language, tradition, knowledge. Religion can have the effect of keeping us apart from our true self, distant from our true self with its dogmas and rituals, instead of revealing our self to ourself. Who are you? Who belongs to a particular religion?

Spirit is what we are in essence and does not need any add-ons, identities or rituals/tradition. You are already whole, complete but you do not know that you are because of the layers of illusion in the way… conditioning, programming, beliefs, ethics, morality, etc. So, the uniqueness of this Lineage is that it emphasizes and uses various tools to remove all the illusory knowledge we have been subjected to. And once this process of undoing has taken place, your true nature that is spontaneous will emerge.

You say you are afraid of losing the security your faith gives you? Where does that fear come from? From the ego mind. But you are not that. You do not exist. You are simply a bundle of concepts, a mere construct. You are the Source. You are divine. You are Spirit. You are not the body-mind. When we rid ourselves of all illusion, we get in touch with who we really are - without identity, the eternal Presence, the Energy, our eternal nature. We are that power within, without which, we cannot do anything. We mistakenly think that we are the doers, but without the engine of Spirit to make things function, we are basically dead bodies.

Be strong and follow your heart

Q. My family's hoping that I return to the Orthodox Church. I try to explain Nonduality to them but they don't understand or respect how important my daily practice is to me.

A. Don't try to explain! It is your practice, your business. Keep it private! It takes courage to leave the Church and go against your parents' wishes. But you are an adult and must follow your inner promptings. The family is always a very challenging, testing ground. But also remember that the family is an illusion. In *Chidananda* we sing... *"No mother no father no brother..."*. Be strong and follow your heart!

Jai Guru! Jai Sadguru!

Further Reading

Selfless Self, (2015, pub. Selfless Self Press) Ed. by Ann Shaw, (also available in French, Spanish, Dutch, Japanese, Korean, Greek, Russian.)

Be With You, (2016, pub. Selfless Self Press) Ed. by Ann Shaw, (also available in French, Spanish, Dutch, Portuguese.)

Ultimate Truth, (2018, pub. Zen Publications, Mumbai.)

Timeless Years With Shri Ramakant Maharaj 2012 – 2022, (2022, pub. Selfless Self Press) Ann & Charles Shaw.

Who Am I?, (2022, pub. Who Am I? Books) Ann Shaw

~~~~~~~~~~~~~~~~~~~~

Resources

Documentary about Shri Ramakant Maharaj:
https://www.annshaw.space/ramakantmaharaj

Shri Ramakant Maharaj Official website:
https://www.ramakantmaharaj.net

Annji Ma Q&A videos:
https://www.annshaw.space/q-a-s-satsangs

About the Author

Ann Shaw has been fascinated with the ultimate questions of "Who am I?" "Where have I come from?" for as long as she can remember. She spent many periods in solitude and reflection, looking for answers. She practised meditation, Self-enquiry, contemplation and also attended various solitary retreats.

Finding out the meaning of life became the most crucial topic. Driven by a fiery determination and in hot pursuit of answers, Ann immersed herself in a wide variety of spiritual literature from east and west. This included the mystics, teachers and masters of varied traditions, including Ramana Maharshi, Paramahansa Yogananda, Joel Goldsmith, Buddhism, Taoism, Rumi and Sufism, etc.

Her interest and passion led her to the academic study of the subjects close to her heart, such as theology, mysticism and comparative religion. Indian Philosophy captivated her, and in particular, Advaita Vedanta. Ann graduated from Edinburgh University's School of Divinity with an MA in 1980. Little did she know then, that her chosen studies, coupled with work experience in the publishing field – and a course in journalism – would all serve her well in the future. When, many years later, Shri Ramakant Maharaj instructed Ann to produce the book *Selfless Self*, she was well equipped with the necessary skills.

Armed with intellectual knowledge and graced with several spiritual/mystical experiences, the search continued with a vengeance. The journey had its highs and lows - with long periods "in the desert", until, at last, further down the illusory road, what she was looking for, found her!

The teachings of Shri Nisargadatta Maharaj and his Master, Shri Siddharameshwar Maharaj, freed Ann from the illusory "I", thus bringing her search to an end. A few years later, during 2013-2014, she spent nearly six months in Nashik, India, with her husband, in the presence of Nisargadatta's successor, Shri Ramakant Maharaj, absorbing the teachings and undergoing the various simple, yet, powerful, practices. She had reached her destination! They remained in close contact with Maharaj over the years, while continuing to spread the teachings across the globe and enabling seekers to visit Maharaj in Nashik.

Auspiciously, Ann returned to Nashik to be with her Master for a few more months in 2018. Shri Ramakant Maharaj attained *Mahasamadhi* in August 31st.

Ann is the editor of *Selfless Self*, (hailed as a spiritual classic), on the teachings of Shri Ramakant Maharaj, which was published in 2015, and has since been translated into eight languages. She also edited Maharaj's books, *Be With You*, (2016) and *Ultimate Truth*, (2018).

Her book *Timeless Years with Shri Ramakant Maharaj 2012 – 2022* by Ann & Charles Shaw was published on March 1st 2022. It is a fascinating story of their time in India with their Master and offers a unique and profound insight into Maharaj's life and the Guru-disciple or

Teacher-student relationship. *Timeless Years* is available in Spanish and is currently being translated into French. *Who Am I?* published on April 11 2022, offers answers to anyone searching for a greater understanding of who we are and why we are here. And not only that, its uplifting, vibrational wisdom enables a true experience of the Self. This self-help book contains practical guidance and techniques on how to know yourself, put an end to suffering and find lasting happiness and peace. *Who Am I?* is a refreshing read that crosses all barriers. Not limited by any belief system, philosophy, religion, spirituality, or genre, it speaks to us all. *Who Am I?* is available in French, Spanish and Hebrew. It is currently being translated into Chinese and will also be published in Japanese.

As well as continuing to write books, she has been invited to travel abroad to spread the teachings - and to offer *Naam Mantra Initiation* - following the instructions of Shri Ramakant Maharaj.

www.ingramcontent.com/pod-product-compliance
Lightning Source LLC
Chambersburg PA
CBHW072151070526
44585CB00015B/1086